PROHIBITION'S PROVING GROUND:

Cops, Cars & Rumrunners in the Toledo-Detroit-Windsor Corridor

By Joseph Boggs

UNIVERSITY OF TOLEDO PRESS

The University of Toledo Press
Toledo, Ohio

2020

The University of Toledo Press
Toledo, Ohio

2020

The University of Toledo Press

www.utoledopress.com

Copyright 2020

By The University of Toledo Press

All rights reserved

Manufactured in the United States of America

Prohibition's Proving Ground:

Cops, Cars & Rumrunners in the Toledo-Detroit-Windsor Corridor

By Joseph Boggs

Edited by Yarko Kuk

Project assistance from Erin Czerniak and Madison Rane Vasko.

Book design by Stephanie Delo

ISBN 978-1-7332664-5-1

Dedication

To all my past, present, and future students.

TABLE OF CONTENTS

Acknowledgements

Simply put, this book would have never been written without the assistance and encouragement of many local librarians, archivists, mentors, colleagues, friends, and family members.

This research journey began at my local public library, the Ellis Library in Monroe, Michigan. The Reference Center staff at Ellis—headed by Louis Komorowski—helped me with unwavering patience and professionalism. Over the span of four years, they must have pulled hundreds of reels of newspaper microfilm and books for me. I'm proud to support this amazing library and the incredible people who work there!

In early 2017, I began to venture beyond my hometown. Along the way, countless archivists and librarians in Ohio, Michigan, and Ontario guided me directly to the primary source materials and resources needed to complete this project. I conducted research at the following libraries, archives, and institutions: the Anti-Saloon League Museum in Westerville, Ohio, the Ohio History Connection Archives, Bowling Green State University's William T. Jerome Library, The University of Toledo's Ward M. Canaday Center, the Toledo-Lucas County Public Library's Local History and Genealogy Department, the Bacon Memorial Library in Wyandotte, Michigan, the Henry Ford's Benson Research

Center, the Detroit Public Library's Burton Historical Collection, Wayne State University's Walter R. Reuther Library, University of Michigan's Bentley Historical Library, University of Windsor's Leddy Library, and the Windsor Public Library's Local History Branch.

I want to particularly thank the entire staff at the Monroe County Museum. Their support during this research project gave me the motivation I needed to see it to the end. A special thanks goes to Caitlyn Riehle, who went on numerous "wild goose hunts" for unique prohibition stories and sources in the Museum's archives, to Gerry Wykes for sharing his background knowledge and personal prohibition expertise, and Andy Clark for allowing me to use my internship at the Museum to further my investigation of prohibition in the Monroe area.

Officer Beth Thieman of the Toledo Police Department and Dr. Shirley Green of the Toledo Police Museum also deserve my sincere gratitude. Officer Thieman opened up the TPD's attic for me, allowing me to analyze and document early prohibition era arrests in Toledo from their historic collection of arrest log books. Dr. Green met with me on numerous occasions to talk prohibition history in the Glass City. She has also lent me numerous books, which I still need to return!

I am particularly indebted to all of the teachers and professors who helped me during my academic career. Dr. Michael Brooks and Dr. Rebecca Mancuso—my thesis advisors at Bowling Green State University—provided much-needed wisdom, timely feedback and academic freedom as I pursued this unique historical topic. Also deserving my thanks are Dr. Scott Martin at BGSU, Dr. Michael Jakobson, Dr. Cynthia Ingham, Dr. Alfred Cave, and Dr. Mary Linehan (all former professors at the University of Toledo), and all my history and English teachers at St. Mary Catholic Central and St. Charles Borremeo.

This book would have never materialized if it were not for Penta Career Center, where I currently teach American History and Psychology. At Penta, my students compel me to consider how the seemingly disparate worlds of history and industry are truly connected. It was through this lens I was able to see how local prohibition enforcement efforts and the automotive environment of the Toledo-Detroit-Windsor corridor fomented a unique historical development in our proverbial backyard. I can not thank Ron Matter, Ed Ewers, Jeff Kurtz, and Ryan Lee for the humbling opportunity to teach our incredible students at Penta. Also, a special thank you goes to Mark Smith, my colleague and friend. I owe all my successes as a teacher to your mentorship.

Most importantly, I need to thank my wife Bridget, my parents Tom and Barb, and my ten siblings Nick, Andrew, Brittany, Jackie, Amanda, Margaret, Tommy, Clare, Anna, and Zeke. Your faith in God and faith in me has sustained me in both good times and bad. Your examples of hard work and humility have made all the difference. I am eternally grateful for your enduring and unconditional love.

Joseph Boggs

Introduction

"Bill and the Water Wagon" was a short story printed in the November 1914 Michigan edition of the *American Issue*, a monthly Anti-Saloon League (ASL) periodical. In this dry parable, Bill, an "average working man," is confronted by an old friend who asks for his view on the "Prohibition question." Admitting he had not thought of it much, Bill surmised, "he would probably vote 'wet'" in the upcoming election "for he was in favor of personal liberty and thought if he wanted to take a drink when he felt like it, it was nobody's business."[1]

On his way home from work that night, a newly painted billboard caught Bill's eye. It boldly proclaimed, "Budweiser is a Friend of Mine." He immediately began to wonder if alcohol companies or the saloons that served intoxicating beverages actually did care for him. Having spent over $1,800 at Tom Kelly's saloon in the past decade, Bill began to realize "he had received nothing of value in return" for his loyalty to the neighborhood-drinking establishment. He remained as "poor as when they move there ten years before."[2]

Bill starts to pay more attention to the saloonkeeper, Tom Kelly, during his "morning pick ups" and drink breaks. He notices that the saloonkeeper wears diamond buttons, lives in a stately mansion, and that he and his wife are always "dressed in the height of fashion." As Bill is enjoying his corncob pipe on his stroll home from work later that night, a "fast roadster" barrels past him. Looking up, Bill recognizes the driver as Kelly. "As he watched Kelly and the automobile disappear down the street it occurred to him that he had handed enough money over Kelly's bar to have bought and paid for an automobile just like the one Kelly had."[3]

This short story was more than just a cautionary tale about the parasitic nature of the alcohol and saloon industries. "Bill and the Water Wagon" embodied how prohibitionists exploited a booming American consumer ethos in their efforts to turn drinkers away from booze. The ASL and other dry leaders were demonstrating to "wets" that their perennial cry of "personal liberty" was getting in the way of personal purchasing power. As in the case of Bill, wages spent at the saloon could instead be diverted towards flashy clothing accessories, an updated wardrobe, or even a better house.

Most conspicuously, this 1914 dry parable notes how Bill's daily drinking routine precluded him from purchasing "an automobile just like the one Kelly had."[4] If any product epitomized the new culture of consumption, it was the automobile. For the first decade of the twentieth century, the "horseless carriage" was just a device of luxury for the elite. Beginning in 1913, however, with Henry Ford's implementation of the assembly line to mass produce the Model T and the subsequent lowering of car prices, the average American wage earner could afford a motor vehicle. Besides the numerous benefits "automobility" provided—including greater access to market goods—the marked uptick in motor vehicle sales spurred a robust automobile culture.

Prohibitionists, or "drys," hoped to utilize this important societal development to change the attitudes and actions of drinkers. Dry organizations like the ASL and the Women's Christian Temperance Union gained momentum and garnered the national spotlight in the late nineteenth century, a couple decades prior to the Ford Motor

Company flooding the American market with its "universal car." By the time widespread passage of local, state, and national prohibition laws were finally realized in the 1910s and 1920s, the precipitous wave of automobile ownership was inundating the country.[5] In turn, drys embraced the motorcar craze of the early twentieth century. They utilized automobiles in public parades to disseminate their anti-alcohol message and traveled in them to deliver speeches in churches and capital buildings. Later, when attempting to defend prohibition, they referenced soaring car production and sales statistics.[6]

Nevertheless, prohibitionists and those who supported their message failed to foresee that the culture of automobility would ultimately play a role in steering the "noble experiment" to its demise. Recent historians have correctly identified the fatal flaw of the Eighteenth Amendment: its inability to be effectively enforced. Specifically, scholars have pointed to abusive and corrupt liquor agents, lack of governmental funding

"Looking up, he noticed that Kelly was driving the machine."

A cartoon from the article "Bill and the Water Wagon" that appeared in the November 1914 edition of *The American Issue*. (Image courtesy University of Michigan, Bentley Historical Library)

and resources, and troubles due to concurrent enforcement.[7] While all of these were indeed problems with policing during the era of prohibition, historians have largely neglected how automobility—the use of automobiles as the major means of transportation—in America fostered a bootlegging culture and presented an array of predicaments to dry enforcers. The jobs of sheriffs, municipal officers, state troopers, and federal agents became more demanding as automobile usage increased in the 1910s. Then in the late 1910s and 1920s, as entrepreneurial rumrunners largely adopted and utilized motor vehicles to transport their illegal cargo, local and national law enforcement was challenged even further.

The Toledo-Detroit-Windsor (TDW) corridor is the ideal place to research how the growing culture of automobility affected dry enforcement. Consisting of Lucas County in northwest Ohio, Monroe and Wayne Counties in southeastern Michigan, and Essex County in southern Ontario, the TDW corridor of the early twentieth century was a microcosm of rapid urbanization, widespread acceptance of the automobile, and prohibition enforcement issues throughout North America. Toledo was growing at a rapid pace, gaining over 70,000 new residents between 1910 and 1920. During the same decade, Detroit rose from the ninth most populous city in America to the fourth most populous. Windsor also witnessed impressive growth, its population nearly tripling from 1901 to 1919.[8] Still, the TDW corridor had its fair share of smaller towns and farming villages like Point Place, Ohio; Erie, Michigan; and Amherstburg, Ontario. The diversity of booming industrial cities, medium-sized county seats, and rural communities within this 60-mile stretch of land provides a nuanced perspective of the prohibition years.

The TDW Corridor was the epicenter of the automobilized world.[9] Detroit rightfully earned its "Motor City" moniker, churning out automobiles at a record-breaking pace throughout the early twentieth century. In 1910, Detroit-based automobile companies produced 63 percent of all cars that made it to market. By 1915, thirteen of the fifteen leading automobile companies listed their primary factories' addresses in the Detroit metro region.[10] Despite being overshadowed by the Motor City's car-making prowess, nearby Toledo also played a formative role in the development of the early American automobile industry. Situated strategically on the western end of Lake Erie, Toledo was a major railroad hub and was uniquely suited for automobile production and distribution. Toledo also had a work force with experience working on cars or in large industrial factories. In 1909 these characteristics enticed John North Willys, President of the Willys-Overland Automobile Company, to select Toledo as the new location for his production facilities. In just a few years of operation, the Willys-Overland Company ranked number two in car sales and journalists reported their automobiles "put Toledo on the map."[11] In Windsor, the Ford Motor Company of Canada flourished under the guidance of Gordon McGregor in the early 1900s. Soon, Windsor became Canada's primary automotive center, attracting numerous motorcar corporations and related businesses.[12]

With Detroit, Toledo, and Windsor mass producing vehicles, residents took advantage of the region's vast and affordable automobile supply. According to a 1917 periodical called "The Ohio Motorist," Lucas County had the third largest number of registered automobiles in the state of Ohio (11,409) behind only Cuyahoga (41,274) and Hamilton (17,199) counties. With one automobile to every seventeen residents, Windsor had the highest per capita car ratio in all of Canada by 1917.[13] Meanwhile, Detroit and its suburbs' automobile registration numbered over 65,000. Collectively, the Toledo-Detroit-Windsor corridor region seems to have only been eclipsed by the New York City metro area in terms of automobiles on the road, but this urban center had a significantly larger proportion of cars operated by chauffeur.[14] In the TDW corridor region, where most of North America's earliest

9

automobile factory workers and motorcar mechanics made their home, a widespread "tinkering" culture emerged and flourished. A.G. Mezerik, an early UAW organizer, moved with his family from the Glass City to the Motor City in 1912. During Mezerik's teen years, he recalled how many Detroiters spent their leisure hours "tinkering" on their cars. Not needing anything too fancy, Midwestern, middle-class folk were perfectly fine with their so-called flivvers, which were the most basic vehicle models. Others essentially built their own automobiles from the ground up. "Kids like me," Mezerik attested, "became expert[s] and bought junk parts to assemble our own Model T's." Countless backyard mechanics along the TDW corridor modified cheap flivvers exactly to their liking. In doing so, local men, women, and even children gained greater mobility and personal freedom on the open road.[15]

Due to unique geographical and geopolitical features of the TDW Corridor, a plethora of prohibition era conundrums affected this region during the late 1910s, 1920s, and early 1930s. Foremost among them, the Detroit River was a porous international boundary that

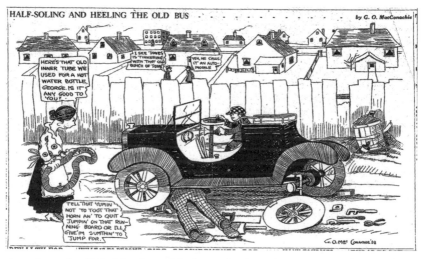

A cartoon by G.O. MacConachie from the March 10, 1918 edition of the *Detroit Free Press* demonstrating the growing trend of people tinkering with their automobiles. (Courtesy the *Detroit Free Press*).

allowed for rampant waterborne bootlegging of liquor from Ontario to Michigan. Several historians—particularly Larry Engelmann, Philip Mason, and Marty Gervais—have extensively covered the soaking wet, dry experience in the Detroit area.[16] Nonetheless, these scholars largely overlooked how the auto-centric bootleggers of the "Motor City" and outlying regions were heavily influenced by the booming local car culture around them. This book demonstrates that the prohibition enforcement problems on the TDW corridor were primarily rooted in the region's widespread embrace of the automobile. To understand how automobility complicated anti-alcohol policies and policing in this region, a thorough analysis of how the TDW corridor came to widely accept the "horseless carriage" is first needed.

---

[1] "Bill and the Water Wagon," *American Issue* (Westerville, Ohio), November 1914.

[2] Ibid.

[3] Ibid.

[4] Ibid.

[5] David E. Ruth, *Inventing the Public Enemy* (Chicago: Chicago University Press, 1996), 38.

[6] Richard Crawford, "Local Effort to Make San Diego Dry Was All Washed Up," *San Diego Union-Tribune*, February 24, 2011, accessed at http://www.sandiegoyesterday.com/wp-content/uploads/2011/03/Anti-Saloonists1.pdf; "Automobiles Instead of Rum," *Brewers Journal and Barley Malt and Hop Trades' Reporter* (New York City: New York), October 1, 1916; "Welcome Pussyfoot Home," *New York Times*, April 25, 1920.

[7] W.J. Rorabaugh, *Prohibition: A Concise History* (New York: Oxford University Press, 2018), 88-89; Lisa McGirr, *The War on Alcohol: Prohibition and the Rise of the American State* (New York: W.W. Norton, 2016), 33; Daniel Okrent, *Last Call: The Rise and Fall of Prohibition* (New York: Scribner, 2010), 141-145; Julien Comte. ""Let the Federal Men Raid": Bootlegging and Prohibition Enforcement in Pittsburgh." *Pennsylvania History: A Journal of Mid-Atlantic Studies* 77, no. 2 (2010), 166-92.

[8] "Population of the 100 Largest Urban Places: 1910 and 1920," *U.S. Bureau of the Census,* accessed at https://www.census.gov/population/www/documentation/twps0027/tab15.txt; *Municipal Statistics: Report on Cities and Towns Having a Population of 10,000 and Over* (Ottawa: Dominion Bureau of Statistics, 1920), 5.

[9] Matthew Daley, "City of Mass Production: Building, Managing, and Living in Detroit, America's First Automobile Metropolis, 1920-1933" (PhD. Dissertation, Bowling Green State University, 2004), 6, 36-37, 46-55.

[10] Brian Palmer, "How Did Detroit Become Motor City?" *Slate*, February 12, 2012.

[11] David A. McMurray, "The Willys-Overland Strike, 1919," *Northwest Ohio Quarterly* (Autumn 1964), vol. 36: no. 4, 173-174; Allen Naldrett, *Lost Car Companies of Detroit*, (Charleston: The History Press, 2016), 68; "Impressions of an Overland-Fest," *Automobile Topics*, June 20, 1912, 427; "Overland Cuts Its Car Prices", *Toledo Blade*, December 5, 1918.

[12] "Factory Development is Setting Fast Pace," *The Windsor Evening Record*, April 9, 1912; David Roberts, *In the Shadow of Detroit: Gordon M. McGregor, Ford of Canada, and Motoropolis* (Detroit: Wayne State University Press, 2006); "Many Motor Cars Made in Canada," *New York Times*, October 7, 1928.

[13] *The Ohio Motorist* (Cleveland: Cleveland Automobile Club, 1917), 22.

[14] Bill Loomis, "1900-1930: The Years of Driving Dangerously" *Detroit News*, April 26, 2015; J. Lewis Robinson, "Windsor, Ontario: A Study in Urban Geography" (MA Thesis, Syracuse University), 50, accessed at https://scholar.uwindsor.ca/cgi/viewcontent. cgi?article=1084&context=swoda-windsor-region.

[15] A.G. & Marie Mezerik Papers, Box 1, Folder 1, Archives of Labor and Urban Affairs, Wayne State University. For more on the automotive tinkering culture that developed in the early 20th century see Kathleen Franz, *Tinkering: Consumers Reinvent the Early Automobile* (Philadelphia: Pennsylvania University Press, 2005).

[16] Larry Engelmann, *Intemperance: The Lost War Against Liquor* (New York: Free Press, 1979); Philip Mason, *Rumrunning and the Roaring Twenties: Prohibition on the Michigan-Ontario Waterway* (Detroit: Wayne State University Press, 1995); Marty Gervais, *The Rumrunners: A Prohibition Scrapbook* (Ontario: Biblioasis, 2009).

CHAPTER 1
The Downsides of Early Automobility: Danger, Death & Crime on the TDW Corridor

On the morning of July 4, 1913, the residents of Wyandotte, Michigan, a small city twelve miles south of Detroit, were readying themselves for a wide range of festivities to commemorate the nation's birth. Starting with a citywide parade at 9:00 a.m., citizens would award monetary prizes for the most festively decorated automobile, most comical float, and "the best appearing rider." Immediately following, the annual motor boat race across the Detroit River and back was scheduled to begin. Next, from 1:30 p.m. to 3:30 p.m. a series of sporting competitions were scheduled including tug-of-war matches between local companies, a "fat man's race," shot-put throw, and even a baseball game pitting a Wyandotte squad against a team from Windsor, Canada. To conclude the day, a band concert would be held in the city park just prior to the riverside firework display at dusk.[17]

The full slate of the day's events was dutifully listed in that morning's *Wyandotte Herald*, the Downriver region's most prominent newspaper. But on this July 4, another front-page article likely diverted readers' attention away from the Fourth of July festivities. As reported, a "motor truck" owned by Wyandotte's Marx Brewing Company nearly ran over a 4-year-old child who suddenly "jumped from the sidewalk." To avoid killing the lad, the driver swerved and was subsequently rear-ended by a street trolley coming up the avenue. The force of the collision threw the automobile against a nearby tree, which was left ravaged by the impact. The brewery's truck finally came to a halt, "impaled on the stump" that remained. Everyone involved in the accident escaped death: the streetcar operator, the two brewery workers, the several local shipyard workers who hitched a ride in the back of the truck, and the youngster.[18]

For many residing within the TDW corridor, this harrowing incident represented much of what was wrong with the growing presence of automobiles in their towns and streets. In the 1910s and 1920s, the motorized vehicles that zoomed by increasingly jeopardized the safety of drivers, unsuspecting pedestrians, and playing children. Many of the statistics in Peter Norton's book *Fighting Traffic* are indeed frightening. From 1918 to 1922, more American pedestrians died from being hit by cars than American soldiers on the battlefields of Europe during World War I. In the 1920s, over 200,000 people were killed in the U.S. because of automobile accidents. Accordingly, a public debate over the uses of the street raged nationwide.[19]

Towns up and down the TDW corridor were concerned for their residents using the streets. Scenarios similar to the accident involving the Marx Brewery truck happened frequently in the region during this era. One incident occurred March 8, 1916 on the outskirts of downtown Toledo in a working-class Polish neighborhood called Lagrinka. Six-year-old Stephen Kowalski, playing near the intersection of Lagrange Street and Central Avenue, "was crushed to death" under the wheels of a truck driven by a Monroe County, Michigan farmer who was delivering fresh meat to the city market. Toledo's coroner quickly designated the horrific occurrence an "accidental death," freeing the local driver from any charges.[20] Just a few days later the *Monroe News Courier*, whose printing offices were less than twenty miles north of the scene of the accident, called for area drivers to slow down near the town's schools. The newspaper suggested signs be put up reading "School property, drive carefully. Preserve the lives of our children."[21]

Due to its high rate of automobile usage, Detroit had significant issues with deadly car accidents. In 1917 alone, motor vehicle crashes killed 129 people in the Motor City, 50 of whom were children under the age of fifteen. Across the river in Canada, Windsor also experienced its share of horrific accidents. One incident, in September 1921, occurred when nine-year-old Thomas Loree hitched a ride just outside of the city. Clinging to the running board of a passing truck, the boy lost his footing and fell in the path of the truck's back wheels. After Thomas' death, the truck driver was investigated by local enforcement.[22]

In 1922, the *Toledo News-Bee* waged a news campaign against

Boys playing "shinny," an older form of street hockey, in Detroit, ca 1910. The surge in the number of vehicles on the roads made such activities hazardous. (Photo courtesy the *Detroit News*).

reckless motorists in the Glass City, publishing a running tally of residents injured or killed by automobiles. By the end of the year, 52 Toledoans had been hit and killed and 471 more had been hurt by motor vehicles. Nevertheless, few cities in North America could compare to the Motor City's notorious reputation for death in the streets. A 1928 study concluded that Detroit had the highest rate of fatality by motor vehicle accident when comparing cities with a population over one million people.[23]

Besides increasing accidents on the road, the democratization of automobiles on the TDW corridor allowed for local criminals to engage in riskier and more profitable illegal endeavors. Prior to widespread motor vehicle ownership, North American bandits' "get-away" options were riddled with limitations. If they hoped to take off on foot, the criminal could not get far nor could they transport stolen or illegal

By the 1920s roads in Detroit and other cities were crammed with automobiles, leading to a rise in accidents and traffic jams. (Photo courtesy the *Detroit News*).

items of considerable size. A horse-drawn buggy allowed a crook to carry off larger items, but at a plodding pace. A passenger railway or trolley system might be quicker, but its very public nature often worked against the criminal's secretive plans. However, once the automobile became increasingly ubiquitous, "a new era of crime" commenced. In 1924, a criminal researcher from Dayton declared that "state lines have been eliminated by the automobile ... In a ride of a few hours criminals can come from distant cities or from neighboring states, commit a crime and disappear while the local authorities are gathering the details of the crime."[24]

Coincidentally, to prove his point about how automobiles eased the escape of lawbreakers, the researcher referenced an example of a daring heist in downtown Detroit. On January 31, 1921, four "desperadoes" pilfered $10,000 worth of liberty bonds from Morton & Company "in the heart of the city during heavy morning traffic." According to a *Detroit Free Press* report, the bandits were so confident in their ability to escape that they waited for several minutes after a Morton employee pushed an alarm button. As three nearby policemen rushed through the door, the robbers easily picked them off with their ready revolvers. They then signaled their driving accomplice to pull up with a "green touring car" and sped off. Witnesses at the scene caught a glimpse of the getaway car's plate, but it turned out that "license number 318-502" had been "stolen several months ago from a Ford machine." The armed robbery "on one of the busiest street intersections in the world" resulted in the death of two officers, precipitated what was then considered Detroit's "greatest manhunt ever," and captured newspaper headlines for the remainder of the year.[25] Several months later, three men were arrested in Chicago with coins and bills that could be traced to the scene of the robbery. Two were sent to the Michigan State Prison in Marquette for life terms while the other served a life term in a Baltimore prison.[26]

Far from being an isolated incident, local newspapers throughout the era reported numerous crimes that were dependent upon motor vehicles, each varying in seriousness and scope. In November 1913, three small-time burglars broke into a department store south of Wyandotte, stole "a quantity of knives, watches, glasses and other small articles." Witnesses reported hearing the sound of an automobile rumbling from the scene.[27]

The "boldest bank robbery that has ever been committed in Monroe County" occurred on September 7, 1919 when armed robbers relieved an Erie bank of $10,000. Nearby residents watched on as the gangsters' Cadillac barreled towards the Michigan-Ohio state line at 70 mph. Toledo arsonists wreaked havoc just after Christmas Day in 1922, setting several apartment buildings and other city structures ablaze. The "firebugs" were said to have fled from each burning location in a Ford sedan.[28]

Hold-up men northeast of Flat Rock, Michigan, who had previously "ousted a Colored man of his fine Buick" in Detroit, held up two local gas stations using their stolen vehicle during the last week of 1926. Across the river in Canada two years later, a bandit held up a Windsor-Toronto express train, entered the mail car, and took specific pieces of mail at gunpoint. As the train slowed, the robber jumped off and sped off in a waiting motor car. These and countless other reports demonstrate how automobiles became seminal accessories to criminal endeavors on the TDW corridor.[29]

Perhaps the most troubling crime throughout the 1910s and 1920s was the theft of automobiles themselves. In their book *Stealing Cars,* historians John A. Heitmann and Rebecca Morales note that the "democratization" of motor vehicles directly resulted in an "epidemic of automobile theft." According to some estimates, one out of every ten American automobiles made in 1920 had been stolen at some point.[30] Despite the advancement of technologies and police departments spending more resources and manpower to tracking down stolen cars, thieves seemed to always be one step ahead.

This was especially true on the TDW corridor, where it was more likely bandits had mechanical experience or worked in the automobile industry. Moreover, *Motor World* magazine noted in 1919 that urban areas situated near state and international lines were "fertile fields for automobile thiefs [sic]. Cars stolen in one state are easily driven across the line and the state in which the car was stolen is powerless." As it might be predicted, the "Motor City" was especially notorious for car thieves, leading all Midwestern and Western American cities in stolen autos in 1919.[31] The nationally syndicated *Automobile Journal* advised travelers to avoid parking their automobiles on certain downtown Detroit streets because that would exponentially raise the risk of having their "cars, tires, and other accessories stolen."[32] In a twelve month period – from July 1, 1917 to June 31, 1918 – 4,069 automobiles were stolen in Detroit for an average of eleven cars taken every day. During that same time period, motor vehicle thefts accounted for over 72 percent of all property stolen in the city.[33]

Toledo was also a hotbed for motor vehicle bandits. Car thefts were such a serious issue in the Glass City that in 1915 C.C. Kilbury of the Toledo Automobile Club told *The Ohio Motorist* that he had crafted a "proposition for the apprehending of automobile thieves." In just a half hour after being notified of a stolen vehicle, Toledo police would be placing pertinent "information in the hands of all garage owners and police departments of 30 cities in every direction."[34]

Automobiles stolen outside of the region also tended to "gravitate towards" the Glass City, likely due to the mechanical expertise of its residents who were engaging in illegal activity. The theft and reconfiguration of stolen automobiles in Toledo had reached such a fever pitch by the summer of 1918 that the Chief of Detectives suggested that local car owners place fifteen to twenty unique marks on their vehicles to prevent them from being targeted.[35]

Besides their use in a broad range of crimes, the democratization of automobiles had other adverse effects on life along the TDW corridor. During the late 1910s and early 1920s, increased motor vehicle usage in the region burdened police departments and challenged pedestrians and older forms of traffic for space on the streets. Law enforcement officials, when they were not dealing with stolen cars or automobile-using absconders, spent more and more time arresting speedsters and investigating deadly traffic accidents. Moreover, motor cars quickly outpaced and replaced electric streetcar lines, in turn eradicating an important mode of regional public transportation and resulting in the loss of interurban jobs. Local newspaper editorials questioned whether automobiles decreased Sunday church attendance as some people chose joyriding over prayer. While some regional booklets boasted that the omnipresence of automobiles was a sign of modernity, some of the region's older citizens lamented the quick disappearance of horse-drawn wagons that plodded through their towns in the previous decades.[36]

[17] "Street Parade! Motor Boat Race, Athletic Sports, Ball Game, Horse Races, Band Concert/Fireworks and Dancing on to Program," *The Wyandotte Herald,* July 4, 1913.

[18] "Motor Truck in Bad Accident," *The Wyandotte Herald,* July 4, 1913.

[19] Peter Norton, *Fighting Traffic: The Dawn of the Motor Age in the American City* (Cambridge: MIT Press, 2008), 25.

[20] "Toledo Boy Killed When Hit by Auto; Driver Not Held," *Monroe News Courier,* March 9, 1916.

[21] "Fast Driving Calls Forth Suggestion—Preserve Children," *Monroe News Courier,* March 14, 1916.

[22] "Two Women Hurt," *Toledo News-Bee*, December 30, 1922; "Motor Deaths are Analyzed," *New York Times*, August 12, 1928.

[23] Bill Loomis, "1900-1930: The years of driving dangerously" *Detroit News*, April 26, 2015, http://www.detroitnews.com/story/news/local/michigan-history/2015/04/26/auto-traffic-history-detroit/26312107/.

[24] Arch Mandel, "The Automobile and the Police", *The Annals of the American Academy of Political and Social Science*, vol. 116, no. 1, 191 - 194.

[25] "Officer Slain, 3 Others Shot in Two Hold-Ups" *Detroit Free Press,* February 1, 1921.

[26] "Second Campus Slayer Given Life Sentence," *Detroit Free Press*, August 5, 1921; "To Try Campus Suspects Here," *Detroit Free Press*, June 7, 1921; "Detectives Shot by 3 Burglars," *Daytona Daily News*, January 31, 1921; "Greatest Man Hunt Detroit Has Ever Witnessed," *The Montreal Gazette*, February 1, 1921; "Accused of Hold-Up; May Be Bank Robber," *New York Times*, February 27, 1921.

[27] "Quarry Store Burglarized", *The Wyandotte Herald*, November 14, 1913.

[28] "One Killed; Five are Hurt in Apartment Blaze," *Toledo News-Bee*, December 27, 1922.

[29] "Hold-Ups Caught in Short Order," *Huron Valley Sentinel*, December 31, 1926.; "Robs Ontario Train; Caught in Detroit," *Detroit Free Press*, October 3, 1928.

[30] "Car Thefts Boost Insurance Rates," *Motor World for Jobbers, Dealers, and Garagemen*, vol. LX, August 27, 1919, 42.

[31] Ibid.

[32] "Detroit Don'ts," *Automobile Journal,* vol. 64, 1917, 23.

[33] "Detroit Thefts Most," *Motor Age*, vol. 34, June 26, 1919, 15; "Bulk of Larcenies are Automobiles", *Detroit Motor News*, vol. 1, July 1918, 19.

[34] "Police Efficiency," *The Ohio Motorist,* 1915, 11.

[35] "Story of a Studebaker Six," *Insurance Newsweek* vol. 21, 1920, p.36. "Mark Your Auto to Foil Thieves," *Toledo News-Bee*, July 1, 1918.

[36] "Cleveland Not So Black As Painted," *Ohio Motorist*, vol. 13, November 1921, 10; "Speeders to Windsor Race Track Warned," *Detroit Free Press*, July 15, 1914; "Automobiles and Church Attendance," *Monroe Evening News*, May 1, 1916; "Covered with Pistol, Auto Speeder Halts," *Detroit Free Press*, August 18, 1917; Larry Engelmann, "O Whisky: The History of Prohibition in Michigan," PhD Dissertation, University of Michigan, 287-290; "Blame Autoists for Car Ills," *Toledo News-Bee*, July 23, 1924; H.W. Gardner, "Windsor, Ontario, 1913, Canada: Including Walkerville, Ford, Sandwich and Ojibway" (1913). SWODA: Windsor & Region Publications, 24, https://scholar.uwindsor.ca/swoda-windsor-region/24 ; "Who Remembers When Local Folks Owned Speedy Nags?", *MEN*, July 26, 1924. According to the the *Ohio Motorist* article, Toledo and Detroit ranked third and fifth in most automobile-caused fatalities in the entire country in 1920.

CHAPTER 2
The Upsides of Early Automobility:
Good Jobs, Good Roads, and Good Times

In spite of all of the downsides of local automobility, motor vehicles became ubiquitous throughout the corridor beginning in the mid-1910s. Henry Ford's implementation of the assembly line in 1913 and the introduction of the $5-a-day wage in 1914 had a lot to do with putting area residents behind the wheel for the first time.[37] As Ford's Highland Park plant began to spit out Model T's in record numbers, local automobile garages began selling more and more "Tin Lizzies."[38] In the subsequent years, other auto factories in Detroit, Toledo, and Windsor adopted similar manufacturing techniques to keep pace, making their cheaper vehicles available to the public. With local auto workers making significantly more money, they now had the ability to purchase the cars they helped produce.[39]

A bountiful supply of cheap flivvers and increased wages for the working middle class may have set the stage for widespread auto ownership in the TDW corridor, but it was not the only reason the region's residents bought motor vehicles. As historians Peter Ling and John Heitmann have both noted, increased economic opportunity, the breaking down of spatial barriers, and new personal freedoms is what drove Americans to purchase the Model T and other cars.[40] Henry Ford went one step further, stating in an interview that automobiles "bring roads, permit people to mingle more freely, increase social intercourse [and] results in business, and the sum total of all is greater public intelligence."[41] These same motivations spurred residents in Toledo, Monroe, Wyandotte, Detroit, Windsor, and locales in between to embrace automobility despite incredible dangers, criminal uses, and other inherent problems.

Indeed, the economic benefits were the primary reason for most acquisitions of a truck or motorcar. Some TDW business owners and entrepreneurs realized these financial upsides earlier than others. The Windsor Trucking & Storage Company, for example, was already established by the late 1800s in its namesake community. When the company added motorized moving vans during the first decade of the twentieth century, business picked up significantly. With their new vehicles, the Windsor Trucking & Storage Company could easily haul household items for a moving family, ship merchandise straight from the train depot to the doorstep, and much more, solidifying itself as a mainstay in southwestern Ontario.[42] Indicating its long-term success, the company continuously advertised in the *Borders City Star* for the first three decades of the twentieth century and its long-time president Fred Allworth purchased a majestic house in Windsor's most fashionable residential district.[43]

Across the Detroit River, many of the Motor City's breweries began utilizing motor trucks to expand their booze business beyond the neighborhood saloon. In 1903, Stroh's Brewery was one of the first to invest in an automobilized fleet, relying less and less on its team of overworked horses that frequently became exhausted on hot summer days or severely injured when falling in icy conditions during the winter months. By 1916, Stroh's had 22 electric and gasoline powered trucks and became famous for its delivery service. Just 60 miles to the south, breweries in the Glass City also began using motor trucks in the mid-1910s.[44] The Huebner Beer Company had six vehicles for "same day delivery" and Krantz Old Dutch advertised a similar service, specializing in delivering crates of 36 bottles of beer. [45]

The use of automobiles for economic benefit was not just confined to the big cities in the region. Nearby small towns, villages, and farming communities increasingly relied upon motor vehicles to make more money or get work done. Downriver in Wyandotte, a drayman named Fred Flock expanded his business in 1917 when he purchased a Model T from his hometown Ford salesman William Pardo. Pardo, who provided a taxi service to expose potential customers to his products, suggested that the drayman supplement his income by using his newly purchased vehicle as a taxi too. Soon, both Flock and his wife were transporting people around town and beyond. [46] In northern Monroe County, farmer Delmont Chapman, Sr. bought a Model T truck in 1920 to haul

Stroh's was one of the first breweries to invest in automobilized trucks for deliveries, boasting a fleet of 22 vehicles by 1916. (Photo courtesy Detroit Public Library, National Automotive History Collection, Burton Historical Collection.)

his produce to Detroit's Eastern Market. With his new motor truck, Chapman reduced the time it took to transport his sweet corn from six hours with his horse and wagon to just 45 minutes. Oddly enough, the farmer actually never mastered how to operate his Tin Lizzie, with its confusing pedal system. His fourteen-year-old son, Delmont Jr., drove it for him. Like hundreds of other teen boys in the region, Delmont Jr. not only possessed his driver's license, but he was enthusiastic about automobiles and learned to "drive it handily." Still, the eighth grader, "a green country boy," was tense about his first haul into the big city. Recalling the motor trek vividly, the sight of policemen along the way was the most nerve-racking portion of the trip for Delmont Jr.[47]

For other residents on the TDW corridor, their motor vehicle's value could not be measured in profits margins or time saved, but more so in the personal freedoms automobility offered. In March of 1924, the *Toledo News-Bee* shared a story of a local married couple, Mr. and Mrs. H.C. Devers, who had taken the trip of a lifetime. After selling their business – The Acme Luxury Shop, at 1408 South Ave. – the Devers hit the road in their "improvised flivver" and drove thousands of miles to the American southwest. Proud of their hometown, the Devers' vehicle was a moving billboard for Toledo, reading: "Good farms, markets. Good industries, wages. Transportations by rail, highway, water. We have everything but climate. Where? Ohio, of course. And you'll do better in Toledo."[48] During their year-long travels, the Devers participated and won first place in the "Tourist Carnival" in San Antonio, Texas. Besides the bold advertisement, judges were apparently impressed with the "cookstove" within the Devers' vehicle. Other newspaper accounts, scrapbooks, and road atlases from the time period attest to the countless cross-country and up-north excursions that regional residents enjoyed.[49]

For people living near the Detroit River, the lure of motoring to and through a "foreign" land was enticing. Accordingly, Windsor and Detroit served as proverbial vacation gateways, with both cities enjoying their fair share of tourists embarking on automobile trips outside their respective countries in the late 1910s and 1920s.

E.A. Cunningham, the chairman of the Touring Committee of Canadian Automobile Association, announced his hopes in 1916 that the "automobilists of Canada" would choose to vacation and spend their money within the "confines of the dominion."[50] This statement not only reflected the growing trend of Canadian motorists visiting destinations in the United States, but also the financial realities of a nation embroiled in a costly overseas conflict. In 1929, border officials at Windsor conducted an informal survey of motoring tourists. American visitors reported a myriad of intended destinations like Toronto, Niagara Falls, and even the distant Maritime provinces. Eight percent of respondents claimed they were planning to stay in Windsor while another fifteen percent "were undecided as to their course." More than 50 percent of tourists agreed on one thing: they "came out of curiosity to see a foreign country."[51]

An increasing selection of affordable automobiles allowed people to travel for leisure. In 1927 a man is pictured in his Willys Whippet at Lake Michigan. (Photo courtesy the Toledo-Lucas County Public Library, Images in Time)

Women in the area also experienced greater freedoms at the dawn of the automobile age despite pervasive negative stereotypes about their driving abilities. As historian Virginia Scharff noted, North American women at the turn of the twentieth century were believed to be "frail, timid, easily shocked, and quickly exhausted" and, as such, were initially steered away from participating in the growing culture of automobility.[52] Yet, as females increasingly defied societal norms and took to the steering wheel in the early 1900s, automakers in the TDW region adjusted, increasingly advertising their vehicles directly to women in order to boost sales. These advertisements in local newspapers, motoring magazines, and other periodicals relied upon gender conventions that cast women as inexperienced drivers and in need of a simplified motorcar. In a 1916 issue of the *Woman's Home Companion*, Toledo's own Willys-Overland Company claimed that its new Model 75 possessed a "clutch which any woman can operate...the steering wheel is large and turns easily."[53] Ten years later, the Walter Wright Chevrolet Sales and Service Garage in Flat Rock, Michigan published a Chevrolet ad in their local newspaper entitled "The Easiest Car for Her to Drive." In order to meet the demands of "feminine approval," the garage boasted that its autos were "easy to start, stop and simple and safe to handle in all conditions."[54]

While the average North American woman undoubtedly had less experience with motor vehicles than her male counterparts, these stereotypical advertisements discounted how the area's booming car industry impacted local women in the TDW corridor. In particular, the region's war production from 1914 to 1918 was a turning point for women's entrance into the wider automobile culture. With young men away at military camps or overseas in European trenches, women were increasingly called upon by automobile companies in Toledo, Detroit, and Windsor to labor in their manufacturing plants. They filled a wide range of positions on factory floors, from sweepers and sorters to drill press operators. The Saxon Motor Company of Detroit even hired seven "girls" full-time as drivers. They transported brand new trucks right off the assembly lines to the shipping docks nearby. Interviewed by reporters with the *Automobile Journal*, all of the women reportedly preferred their new job over previous ones, and they certainly "would not trade it for a place at the kitchen sink or at the firing end of a sewing machine." Women office workers at Saxon were said to be "envious," planning to "quit their jobs and get into the driving positions."[55]

The conclusion of the "Great War" marked the beginning of a new era for North American women. Beyond the passage of suffrage laws in Canadian provinces, America's ratification of the Nineteenth Amendment in 1920, and the general advancement of female rights, women also re-imagined their roles in society and challenged the norms that previously dictated their behavior. The so-called "New Woman" thought differently about their interactions with motor vehicles. Rather than just a vehicle for leisure or elevating one's status, automobiles were increasingly perceived to be a practical device for the rapidly changing economic system. At the 1919 Detroit Automobile Show, much to the surprise of observers, female attendees mostly passed over the flashy "limousines and racy roadsters" on display, the *Detroit Free Press* noted that it was "going to be a long, long trail for the feminine mind to get back to where it was before the war." Women working and living in the region, as the newspaper revealed, had become accustomed to the "stern, serious business" of trucking, hauling, and related transportation costs. Accordingly, the thousands of women in attendance at the auto show "arranged themselves prettily about the trucks and trailers and tractors and discussed them in learned fashion and with the frank understanding of fellow servants in a common cause."[56]

In December 1920, University of Michigan professor W.D. Henderson visited Monroe to deliver a lecture entitled "The New World and The New Woman." Unsurprisingly, one of his major contentions was that WWI had transformed the lives of American females. "The war set women free, and made it possible for them to enter into any line of industry, and wear any garb that the industry called for," Henderson claimed. "She is no longer bound down by custom."[57] Customs that previously restrained local women from working in the auto industry or getting behind the wheel, by and large, had been significantly diminished. By 1921, 3,383 Detroit women worked as "semi-skilled operatives" and many more as unskilled laborers in automobile factories. An additional 35 women found employment as chauffeurs in the Motor City.[58] A brief passage in a 1919 magazine article also reveals the surge of female drivers in the region following the Great War. Besides noting that several deaf men and those who had "participated in fatal accidents" had been stripped of their driving privileges, an estimated 40,000 to 50,000 women were reported to be driving without licenses in the Detroit area.[59]

The same magazine article mentioned further how more than 100 young males aged 14- to 16-years-old had acquired their first licenses.[60] An

A number of Ford Model T automobiles in front of the Upp Motor Company, at the corner of Detroit Avenue and Collingwood Boulevard in Toledo, ca 1923. (Photo courtesy the Toledo-Lucas County Public Library, Images in Time)

inspector at the Detroit office was apparently impressed by the "unusual ability and proficiency" these boys displayed behind the wheel.[61] This example reflected larger developments on the TDW corridor: teenagers driving and taking advantage of the area's culture of automobility. Some youngsters, such as Delmont Chapman, Jr, acquired their licenses and worked as delivery boys for regional businesses or farms. Others learned the basic mechanics of cars by joining local automobile garages as young apprentices there to "pick a machine to pieces." A.G. Mezerik remembered fondly how he and neighborhood friends in Detroit "could stand with our backs to the streets and name the cars by the sound they made."[62] Yet, for some area teens, the numerous automobiles in their midst seemed like low-hanging, forbidden fruit. High school-aged boys and girls frequently borrowed cars without permission and took them for "joy-rides" into the surrounding countryside. To the ire of parents and the morally inclined in the community, "petting parties" and "highway love nests" often formed.[63]

By the early 1920s, a regional automobile culture connecting Toledo, Detroit, and Windsor was firmly established and reaching all segments of society. In turn, towns and villages in between quickly embraced the motorcar as well. As early as June 1914, Monroe businessmen were embarking on organized long distance "automobile trips" through Toledo and points further south. Each individual was "to wear a linen duster" and "decorate his car according to his own ideas."[64]

That same year, Monroe's Van Blerck Motor Company helped the city modernize its fire department. "Little did we think a year or two ago, when the city council was talking about buying an auto-truck fire engine, that the time was right at hand when the motors which furnish power for these monsters were to be a product of our own Floral City," declared one local newspaper. "However, this is now the case, and the beautiful and very effective fire engine...is driven by a 100-horsepower, high-speed Van Blerck motor."[65]

Sales and repair garages in Wyandotte, Michigan, Walkerville, Ontario, and Maumee, Ohio – as evidenced by their annual directories – flourished in the 1910s and 1920s. An early resident of Toledo's first gated community, Birckhead Place, attempted to fight the advancement of automobile garages in his neighborhood. In 1914, home owner Charles Fox claimed the construction of a garage violated local deed agreements. The developers argued those early restrictions were meant to keep out farm animals. Fox subsequently sued the developers and the case reached the Ohio Court of Appeals. Fox's lawsuit was rejected and the age of the automobile began in one of the Glass City's finest neighborhoods.[66]

For townspeople living in places like Ida and Petersburg in rural Monroe County, newspaper reports indicated that they too participated in the growing culture of automobility. Often traveling to the nearest salesroom, these rural residents took a test drive of the car models they were interested in, purchased their first automobile, and had it subsequently delivered to their residence or farm. By the mid to late 1920s, many of these rural villages would have their own garages. The frequent accident reports coming from these locales further illustrate the widespread embrace of motorcars in outlying areas.[67]

The "Good Roads" movement was also essential to the development of a regional automobile culture. Beginning in the late 1800s with the rise of the bicycle, American citizens began to clamor for the widespread improvement of roads, and for good reason: The vast majority of roads were not only impassable during wet seasons but also quite narrow and filled with hazardous ruts. As the motorcar grew in popularity during the first two decades of the twentieth century, miles of streets around Toledo, Detroit, and Windsor were widened, paved, and straightened.[68]

The improvement of one road in particular, however, played an integral role in creating a sense of region in the TDW corridor. The Dixie Highway was actually a series of connected roads stretching from

Miami, Florida, through Toledo, along the western edge of Lake Erie into Detroit, then on to the northern tip of Michigan. The local Dixie Highway referred to the area between the Glass City and the Motor City. A *Detroit Free Press* article noted that the Monroe County portion of the Dixie had long been a "weak link" and a "barrier to highway traffic" well before the automobile age.[69] Only "travelable a few months of the year," the Toledo and Detroit Automobile Clubs, along with prominent local politicians and businessmen, began to raise funds and gather support to pave the entire stretch from Toledo to Detroit.[70] Further hastened by the need for a reliable road in order to transport wartime vehicles manufactured in local factories, the Dixie Highway in Monroe County was finally completed in the fall of 1918.[71]

Elaborate festivities underscored the significance of the opening of the newly paved Dixie. On October 15, 1918, the mayors of Detroit and Monroe, Toledo's vice-mayor, numerous representatives of regional automobile clubs, and many other distinguished men gathered at the

A muddy, rutted Dixie Highway runs through LaSalle, Michigan, before being paved in 1918. (Photo courtesy the Monroe County Museum Archives)

southern bank of the Huron River in South Rockwood, Michigan. A local boy and girl dressed as Uncle Sam and Lady Columbia cut the ceremonial ribbon together, opening the concrete highway to future travel. The mayors and vice-mayor also wielded a "golden spade," collectively shoveling off a pile of mud that represented the poor road conditions of the past. The group then proceeded with an army convoy to the city of Monroe where numerous lofty speeches were spoken and a grand luncheon was held.[72]

Within weeks of its completion, an automobile journal was already calling the Dixie "one of the most heavily traveled highways in the United States." A traffic census taken less than a year later confirmed just how many cars and trucks were utilizing the newly paved road. On one day alone, May 29, 1920, the Monroe County Highway Engineer and his crew counted 3,353 vehicles passing by in the southbound lane. Of those automobiles, 56 percent were "foreign" and 211 trucks and nineteen loaded trailers took advantage of the Dixie to haul goods to nearby Toledo. Another census was taken the following year for the Dixie Highway and it demonstrated that the flow of motorcars was only increasing. Official counts indicated "5,661 vehicles passed over the south end of the highway and 4,550 on the north end."[73] In creating a "good road" connecting the Motor City to the Glass City, commercial enterprises and small local businesses had greater access to nearby urban populations and therefore greater economic opportunities. Even Windsor shops benefited from the completion of the Dixie. As more automobilists traveled to Detroit for business or pleasure by way of the Dixie Highway, travelers opted to cross the river and spend their money in Canada.[74]

Beyond the growing presence of flivvers on highway stretches, backcountry roads and downtown streets, perhaps the most important effect of the regional motorcar industry was in providing employment opportunities for thousands of locals. By 1920, 60,000 Detroiters made their living in automobile factories and thousands more worked in car accessory industries.[75] Five year later, the Ford Motor Company alone employed over 108,000 locals in its legendary Highland Park and River Rouge factories.[76] Across the river in Canada, an estimated 40 percent of all workers living in Windsor, Ford City, and Walkerville labored at Ford Motor Company of Canada or its suppliers. In Toledo, the Willys-Overland automobile company was the city's largest employer with 15,000 workers in 1918.[77] A decade later, Willys-Overland was still the Glass City's top employer, with the next three leading companies primarily concerned with manufacturing or selling automobile parts.[78] Many residents living in the TDW corridor depended on the region's booming automobile industry for their income.

In the 1910s and 1920s, the TDW corridor had become a thoroughly autmobilized region. Many locals purchased their first cars and enjoyed driving them on newly improved roads in the area and beyond. Urban and rural businessmen realized how motorized trucks and flivvers created greater economic opportunities and access to distant markets. Residents throughout the TDW corridor often relied upon the booming automobile industry for employment. Despite the numerous downsides and predicaments that motorcars presented to local communities and

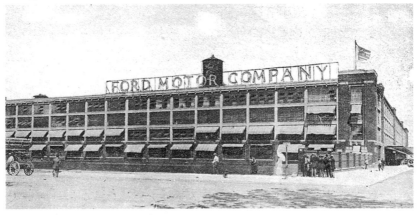

The Ford Motor Company's Highland Park plant, ca 1915. (Image courtesy the University of Windsor, Leddy Library)

streets, the personal freedom afforded by automobile ownership and the financial benefits that resulted from the region's automobile industry would not be overlooked by the area's residents and businessmen. Just as the TDW corridor had come to fully embrace the motorcar, another major development would forever change the sentiments and behaviors of the region. A movement to dry out the TDW corridor was gaining momentum.

[37] Matt Anderson, "Ford's Five Dollar Day," January 3, 2014 https://www.thehenryford.org/explore/blog/fords-five-dollar-day/.

[38] Steven Watts, *The People's Tycoon: Henry Ford and the American Century*, (New York: Vintage, 2005), 276.

[39] "Willys Overland in Full Production," *Automotive Industries*, vol. 40, June 26, 1919; David Roberts, *In the Shadow of Detroit: Gordon M. McGregor, Ford of Canada, and Motoropolis* (Detroit: Wayne State University Press, 2006), 100.

[40] John Heitmann, *The Automobile and American Life* (Jefferson, North Carolina: McFarland & Co., 2009), 44, 87-100; Peter J. Ling, *America and the Automobile: Technology, Reform and Soical Change, 1893-1923* (Manchester: Manchester University Press, 1990), 20-23

[41] "Business is Sound, Ford Says," *Toledo News-Bee,* November 30, 1925.

[42] "Windsor, Ontario, 1913, Canada: Including Walkerville, Ford, Sandwich and Ojibway" (1913). SWODA: Windsor & Region Publications, 50, https://scholar.uwindsor.ca/swoda-windsor-region/24.

[43] "A Walking Tour of Victoria Avenue," Windsor Architectural Conservation Advisory Committee, 9-10; Edwina DeWindt, *Proudly We Record: The Story of Wyandotte, Michigan* (Wyandotte Rotary Club, 1985), 113-114.

[44] "Electric-Vehicle Practice of Larger Brewery," *Electrical Review,* vol. 68, 1916, 16-20.

[45] Arnette Hawkins, "Raising Our Glass: A History of Saloons in Toledo, 1880-1919" (Master's Thesis, University of Toledo, 2004), 144.

[46] Edwina Dewindt, *Proudly We Record: The Story of Wyandotte, Michigan*, 113-114.

[47] Delmont Chapman, interview by Jim Miller, March 10, 1978, in South Rockwood Michigan, transcript, Monroe County Community College Oral History Collection, Ellis Library, Monroe, Michigan; Delmont Chapman, interview by Penny Dicks, March 7, 1990, in South Rockwood Michigan, transcript, Monroe County Community College Oral History Collection, Ellis Library, Monroe, Michigan.

[48] "Travelers Spread Word of Hometown's Greatness," *Toledo News-Bee,* March 22, 1924.

[49] "Chief On Trip," *Monroe Evening News*, September 15, 1921; "Erie," Monroe Evening News, July 18, 1924; "H.T. Talbot's 1928 Auto Road Atlas of the United States and Eastern Canada," author's personal collection; Gustave Beck's Scrapbook, circa 1910-1930, Monroe County Museum Archives, Monroe Michigan.

[50] "Canada Expects Big Motor Year," *New York Times*, May 30, 1926.

[51] "Tourists Say Scenery is Lure of Canada," *New York Times*, September 6, 1929.

[52] Virginia Scharff, *Taking the Wheel: Women and the Coming of the Motor Age* (Albuquerque: University of New Mexico Press, 1991) 2.

[53] Overland Advertisement, *Woman's Home Companion,* January 1916, 26-27.

[54] "The Easiest Car for Her to Drive," Advertisement *The Huron Valley Sentinel,* December 10, 1926.

[55] "Women Working in Factories," *The Automobile*, vol. 36, June 28, 1917, 1268; "U.S. Makers Build Plants in Canada," *The Automobile*, vol. 36, June 21, 1917, 1175; Giving Motor Cars the Final Road Test in Driveaways," *Automobile Journal*, vol. 65, June 10, 1918, 8-9. Toledo women were also being recruited and taught to drive Ford vehicles for the local Red Cross a month before America's entry into WWI, see "Girls Want to Drive Auto If We Go to War," *Toledo News-Bee*, February 17, 1917.

[56] "Trucks Appeal at Auto Show," *Detroit Free Press*, March 4, 1919.

[57] "Lecture was Greatly Enjoyed," *Monroe Evening News*, December 9, 1920.

[58] "Machinists Lead Detroit Workers," *Detroit Free Press*, December 16, 1921.

[59] "Auto Drivers' Licenses, *The Indicator*, vol. 45, August 5, 1919, 243.

[60] Ibid.

[61] "Youths Form Club to Steal Cars," *Automobile Topics*, vol. 32, December 27, 1913, 503.

[62] "Study of Motor Cars Fascinating," *Detroit Free Press*, March 29, 1914.

[63] "Sheriff to Break Up Highway Love Nests," *Toledo News-Bee*, October 27, 1922; "Petting Parties are Blamed for Youthful Crime," *Detroit Free Press*, January 29, 1924; "Indecent 'River Parties' Stir Mayor to Action," *Detroit Free Press*, August 14, 1924; "Petting Parties in Auto Taboo," *Lansing State Journal*, November 12, 1926.

[64] "Local Happenings", *Monroe Record Commercial*, June 18, 1914; "Local Happenings," *Monroe Record Commercial*, June 11, 1914.

[65] "A Modern Automobile Fire Truck—Van Blerck Equipped," *Record Commercial*, August 6, 1914.

[66] "Toledo's First Gated Community Turns 100," *Toledo Blade*, March 11, 2007.

[67] "Windsor, Ontario, 1913, Canada: Including Walkerville, Ford, Sandwich and Ojibway" (1913). SWODA: Windsor & Region Publications; "1916 Vernon's City of Windsor Directory," SWODA: Windsor & Region Publications; "The Downriver Directory," 1915, Bacon Memorial District Library Archives, Wyandotte, Michigan; "Barbour's New Idea Directory of Wyandotte, Ford City, and Grosse Ille, and Farms on Mail Routes," 1921, Bacon Memorial District Library Archives, Wyandotte, Michigan; Maumee Village Directory," June 1, 1927, Lucas County Public Library Local History Archives, Toledo, Ohio; "Maumee Village Directory," June 15, 1929, Lucas County Public Library Local History Archives, Toledo, Ohio; "New Automobile Owners," *Monroe Evening News,* July 8, 1916; Interview with Harold Stotz, Interviewed by Mark Metz, January 31, 1996, *Monroe County Community College Oral Histories*, Monroe County Museum Archives.

[68] John Heitmann, *The Automobile and American Life* (Jefferson, North Carolina: McFarland, 2009), 73-75; "Border Towns Will Be Linked in New Highway," *Detroit Free Press,* September 9, 1917; "Essex Club Gets Busy," *Detroit Motor News*, vol. 1, 1918, 27; "Wayne County Builds Roads," *DFP,* August 4, 1918; "Work on Highway to Begin in Spring," *Detroit Free Press*, November 29, 1918; "Essex to Spend More than $650,000 on Roads," *Detroit Free Press*, March 20, 1921; "Detroit Makes Record in Concrete Paving," *Detroit Free Press*, July 31, 1927.

[69] Monroe Road is Weak Link," *Detroit Free Press*, March 24, 1918.

[70] "Toledo Raises Funds," *The Ohio Motorist*, vol. 7, 1915, 18.

[71] "Automobile World," *Detroit Free Press* April 29, 1918; "Detroit-Monroe Road Opens on October 15 if Nothing Happens," *Detroit Free Press*, September 22, 1918.

[72] "Dixie Highway is Now Opened," *Detroit Free Press*, October 16, 1918.

[73] "Increased Traffic Over Last Year", *Monroe Evening News*, August 25, 1921.

[74] "Motorists Renew Border Relations," *Detroit Free Press*, January 19, 1919.

[75] "Machinists Lead Detroit Workers," *Detroit Free Press,* December 16, 1921; "Thousands Are Given Steady Employment in Accessory Plants," *Detroit Free Press,* November 27, 1922;

[76] "Ford Now Employs 161,000," *New York Times*, May 31, 1925.

[77] David Roberts, *In the Shadow of Detroit: Gordon M. McGregor, Ford of Canada, and Motoropolis* (Detroit: Wayne State University Press, 2006), 260; "Overland is Biggest Auto Plant," *Toledo News-Bee*, July 18, 1914.

[78] David A. McMurray, "The Willys-Overland Strike, 1919," *Northwest Ohio Quarterly* vol. 36, Autumn 1964, 174; "Toledo Leadership: Manufacturing in Toledo," 1929, in Toledo Industries Pamphlets Folder, Monroe County Museum Archives.

CHAPTER 3
Drinking & Barroom Culture
on the TDW Corridor

Following in the footsteps of her famous mother, Laura Ingalls Wilder, Rose Wilder Lane secured a writing assignment that many 30-year-old journalists could only dream of: penning the first biography of the world-famous automobile magnate Henry Ford. As indicated by the title, *Henry Ford's Own Story: How a Farmer Boy Rose to the Power that Goes with Many Millions, Yet Never Lost Touch with Humanity*, Wilder Lane had embraced the folk hero persona that Ford had carefully crafted. In the biography's foreword, the author proclaimed, "With millions piling upon millions in our hands, most of us would lose our viewpoint. He [Ford] has kept his—a plain mechanic's outlook on life and human relations. He sees men all as parts of a great machine, in which every wasted motion, every broken or inefficient part, means a loss to the whole."[79]

In the process of writing the book, Wilder Lane discovered what the industrialist believed to be one of the primary causes for these "broken and inefficient part[s]." Ford told her "I have never tasted liquor in my life... I'd as soon think of taking any other poison." Ford's enmity for booze was already well known among his employees and the residents of the region. Still, Wilder Lane doubted the veracity of this claim. "In those early days of Detroit he must have experimented at least once with the effects of liquor on the human system," wrote the author.[80]

Wilder Lane was not attempting to diminish the moral character of Henry Ford. Instead, she was illustrating how drinking had become synonymous with Detroit and the region. In fact, the consumption of alcohol on the TDW corridor was as old as many of the area's most prominent cities and towns. The French founder of Detroit, Antoine Laumet de La Mothe Cadillac, earned much of his income by setting up an alcohol-trading network among the Native Americans on both sides of the Detroit River. During his first campaign for office, Hazen Pingree, legendary mayor of late nineteenth century Detroit, visited the city's ethnic bars regularly, corralling just enough votes to secure a slim electoral victory.[81]

Before the incorporation of Toledo in 1836, saloons and taverns served residents and travelers along the Maumee River. From 1897 to 1904, Toledo's Mayor Samuel "Golden Rule" Jones initiated a "safekeeping" policing policy for non-violent inebriates. Instead of being charged and fined for "drunken and disorderly" conduct, tipsy Toledoans or intoxicated visitors to the Glass City could count on spending a worry-free night in the city jail and released without penalty in the morning. The practice of safekeeping drunkards would continue in Toledo until World War I.[82]

Visitors to the Windsor area throughout the 1800s commented on the profusion of hard cider being manufactured and consumed by both men and women. The nearby town of Walkerville, which would later be absorbed into the city of Windsor, was essentially the by-product of Hiram Walker's incredible success as a distiller of Canadian Club whiskey.[83]

By the 1910s, when Wilder Lane was conducting background research on Ford and the region in which he grew up, saloons and breweries dotted the TDW landscape. In 1913, Detroit had 1,530 barrooms and at the onset of prohibition, the Motor City possessed seventeen breweries.[84] Despite the fact that stand alone saloons were outlawed in Ontario in 1897, the greater Windsor area in 1916 had 40 booze-serving hotels and inns, seven wine and liquor wholesalers, two breweries, and one distillery. It was well known throughout the province that Windsor had "far more [liquor] licenses proportionately than in other cities in Ontario."[85] Toledo, known for its pervasive drinking culture, had 408 saloons and five breweries in 1918.[86]

Pre-prohibition drinking establishments and businesses provided many services and benefits to their patrons, communities, and even the nation as a whole. Saloons in the TDW region were no exception. In

Fred Christian's Saloon on Navarre Avenue in east Toledo, ca 1880. (Photo courtesy the Toledo-Lucas County Public Library, Images in Time)

1918, the Reverend John H. Phelan and the Department of Sociology at Toledo University conducted a "scientific and analytical" study of the saloons in Toledo in 1918. "The Saloon as a Phase of Commercialized Amusements in Toledo," though a thorough study, was certainly biased against the existence of drinking establishments. The researchers visited all 408 licensed saloons in the city, spending 30 minutes at each one. They took note of seemingly trivial aspects of barroom culture including the use of profane language, police gazettes scattered on tables, and even the window blinds utilized to "shut out the public view." Phelan was particularly disgusted at the poor conditions of the saloons' restrooms. "The condition of the toilets in many of the public saloons is a subject demanding community attention," wrote the Toledo minister. Undoubtedly, many Glass City bars needed to improve their restroom facilities, which were often placed in dingy, dark, and damp basements. Phelan nevertheless acknowledged that Toledo had very few public restrooms but failed to credit the saloons for providing toilets free of charge to its visitors.[87]

Despite being a mostly critical report, a close analysis of Phelan's study does reveal how the surrounding community benefited from Toledo's saloons. Perhaps the most obvious benefit was that 371 of the 408 drinking establishments possessed dining rooms, restaurants, or lunch counters. The study notes these features not only provided quality food to Glass City residents and workers, but they were one of the few places that economic or social status did not matter. Phelan recorded that these barroom eateries were "patronized indiscriminately by laboring men, clerks, and well-to-do business men." Further, Toledo's saloons were gathering places for both migrant groups and labor unions. The study noted that while 49 percent of the bars analyzed were visited by "mixed" nationalities, the remaining 51 percent were decidedly ethnic. Polish, German, Bulgarian, Greek, Irish, Black, Jewish, and Italian saloons were dispersed throughout the city. For those new to the Toledo, a common

ABOVE: A pair of horse-drawn brewery wagons in East Toledo, ca 1900. (Photo courtesy the Toledo-Lucas County Public Library, Images in Time) BELOW: Brewery wagons were replaced by motorized trucks like this one used by Diekman Bottling Works in Monroe. (Photo courtesy the Monroe County Museum Archives)

space where others spoke the same languages or dialects and shared the same customs was comforting to immigrants and migrants alike. The 129 local unions also could count on their neighborhood saloons to provide meeting rooms for "the lowest possible rents, and often free," according to the study. Finally, the study revealed that women frequently found employment within Toledo's drinking establishments, with 232 of the saloons having female servers and 67 owned outright by female proprietors.[88]

Other sources demonstrate how the region's saloons, breweries, and distilleries benefited residents in other noticeable ways. Charles D. Williams, an Episcopalian bishop in Detroit, declared in a meeting with other dry ministers that "poverty more frequently drives men to drink than drink drives men to poverty."[89] Williams noted that while he still would be voting dry for the upcoming state prohibition measure he also believed Detroit's saloons served as "poor man's club[s]," offering comfort and stability to residents who needed it most.[90] One *Toledo News-Bee* article attested to the fact that many of the city's workers relied upon neighborhood saloons to cash their weekly checks because banks often only had locations downtown.[91] Soon after Canada's sudden entrance into the "Great War" in 1914, the Hiram Walker Distillery in Walkerville donated $50,000 to the Minister of Finance in Ottawa, hoping to set a precedent for other large companies throughout the country. [92]

Despite these noted benefits, the region's drinking culture was portrayed in local newspapers as a source of widespread drunkenness, despair, vice, and criminality. Some drunkards became small-time celebrities because of the frequency in which their names appeared in the local press. A Windsor man who went by the name of "Tin Can" Murphy became infamous for the number of drunk and disorderly charges he accumulated.[93] Other stories from the time period document how area women were consistently affected by neighborhood saloons over-serving their husbands. One Detroit woman said her often intoxicated husband,

The rack warehouse at Hiram Walker & Sons, in Walkerville, ca 1900-1910.
(Photo courtesy the Library of Congress, 2016811832)

besides wasting his wages on booze, would stumble home drunk from local poolrooms, use threatening language, and pinch her until she was "black and blue" if she refused his "loving advances."[94] One instance across the river, however, flipped the traditional barroom script. The *Detroit Free Press* reported that one housewife admitted to the Windsor police court that "her weakness for drink caused her to neglect the home and spend the money her husband provided for herself and children in saloons."[95]

Local newspapers also frequently portrayed area imbibers as helpless and hopeless fools. In 1917, an inspector working for the state of Ohio went undercover in a Toledo drinking establishment called the Stifter Café. He reported it was "the worst that had come under his observation" in four years of work.[96] There he witnessed numerous females so heavily intoxicated that they could not walk out of the saloon upright. As drunkards ended up on the streets at closing time, they were sometimes taken advantage of, or worse. One young Detroit man named Joseph Dude "visited several bar rooms too many" and by the end of the night had all of his personal belongings and even his clothes taken from him by "unsympathetic and mercenary" thieves.[97] Another Detroit man suspected of intoxication was found dead in the streets by a police patrol wagon.[98] Regional newspapers printed stories of suicidal drinkers, some taking their lives in the saloon or while they were incarcerated. Journalists were sure to note whether or not the drunken deceased left behind a wife and children, once again characterizing—perhaps rightfully so—alcohol as a destroyer of families.

Area saloons frequently became synonymous with illicit activities like gambling and prostitution. Bars in the Tenderloin districts in both Detroit and Toledo often contained dice dens and street women within. While some alcohol-serving Windsor hotels and poolrooms were actually "disorderly houses," others were apparently "honeycombed with gambling," as declared by one concerned local pastor.[99] In 1914, Detroit police raided a handful of city saloons, tearing out "stalls and booths" that promoted the "delinquency" of females.[100] Toledo's Tenderloin district was especially notorious, prompting one historian to claim it was a location "where thieves, gamblers, grafters, sporting women, degenerates and drunks ran free."[101] With 35 houses of ill repute, dozens of booze-serving gambling joints, and over 1,000 prostitutes, the Glass City's vice district was a topic of continuous controversy for much of the 1910s.[102]

A War Department directive ultimately settled the fate of Tenderloin districts across the country, including Toledo's. As the fighting in the trenches raged on overseas, the American government needed a fresh supply of ready and able young men to take up arms. To ensure that their "doughboys" were fit for battle, cities across the United States were strongly encouraged to shut down their respective red light districts. Toledo's "clean-up" date was May 1, 1918 and one *Toledo News-Bee* journalist described the scene:

> No better night could have been chosen for the passing of the Tenderloin. Rain swept the streets where the refuse which had accompanied the moving-out of some of the places during the day, was still scattered. Thru the cold mist, the lights of passing autos made yellow halos and the electric globes above the doorways of the houses blinked in a sinister manner. A few men loitered along sheltering walls. Cats, abandoned in the Tuesday exodus of the women, slunk thru the rain. Houses, where a few nights before there had been music and laughter, were silent. By midnight the lights above the doors of the houses had all gone out. Behind drawn blinds even the lamps were darkened. Notorious resorts were deserted and lowered heavily over the dismal streets.[103]

Newspapers also linked saloon culture to recurrent episodes of violent crime in the region. The *News-Bee* and *Free Press* of the 1910s regularly shared front-page stories of armed robberies and shooting deaths in

Toledo's and Detroit's drinking establishments. One neighborhood Detroit saloon was aptly nicknamed "Bucket of Blood" due to the continuous fights, murders, and "the number of night sticks" that were reportedly "cracked over belligerent skulls" by cops stationed at the location. Another Detroit bar received negative press and was threatened with the loss of its license after a woman was "brutally beaten" on the premises.[104] Windsor area newspapers did not publish nearly as many stories on violence within their own drinking establishments.[105] Instead, they tended to complain about their countrymen who engaged in the criminal culture pervading Detroit saloons or who became the victims of crime within these nearby bars just across the river.[106]

---

[79] Rose Wilder Lane, *Henry Ford's Own Story: How a Farmer Boy Rose to the Power that Goes with Many Millions, Yet Never Lost Touch with Humanity* (New York: Forest Hills, 1917), v-vi.

[80] Ibid, 28.

[81] Larry Engelmann, "O, Whisky: The History of Prohibition in Michigan," Dissertation, University of Michigan, 1971, 49; John Schneider, *Detroit and the Problem of Order, 1830-1880: A Geography of Crime, Riot, and Policing* (Lincoln, Nebraska: University of Nebraska Press, 1980), 92-95, 112-115.

[82] Arnette Hawkins, "Raising Our Glass: A History of Saloons in Toledo, 1880-1919," 19-21; "Toledo's Reorganized Police Force," *The National Police Journal*, March 1919, 3-5.

[83] Patrick Brode, *Dying for a Drink*: *How a Prohibition Preacher Got Away with Murder* (Biblioasis: Windsor, 2018), 20-21; Marty Gervais, *The Rum-runners: A Prohibition Scrapbook* (Biblioasis: Windsor, 2009), 33-37.

[84] Peter H. Blum, *Brewed in Detroit: Breweries and Beers Since 1830* (Wayne State University Press: Detroit, 1999), 313-318.

[85] "1916 Vernon's City of Windsor Directory," SWODA: Windsor & Region Publications; "License Reduction," *Windsor Evening Record*, October 12, 1912.

[86] Arnette Hawkins, "Raising Our Glass: A History Saloons in Toledo, 1880-1919," 161.

[87] John J. Phelan, "The Saloon as a Phase of Commercialized Amusements in Toledo," *Social Survey Series*, June 1918, 13, 18, 21.

[88] Ibid.

[89] Madelon Powers, *Faces Along the Bar: Lore and Order in the Workingman's Saloon, 1870-1920* (Chicago: University of Chicago Press, 1998).

[90] Roy Rosenzweig, *Eight Hours For What We Will: Workers & Leisure in an Industrial City, 1870-1920* (London: Cambridge University Press, 1983); "Says Saloon is Poor Man's Club," *Detroit Free Press*, May 6, 1916;

[91] "Thousands in Checks Cashed by Saloonist," *Toledo News-Bee*, April 9, 1917

[92] "Walker Company Gives $50,000 for British War Fund," *Detroit Free Press*, August 28, 1914.

[93] "Still Drunk," *Windsor Evening Record*, December 3, 1913.

94 "Gene in Saloon Too Much, Wife Claims," *Detroit Free Press,* March 21, 1914; "Wife Beater Given Term Behind Bars," *Detroit Free Press,* August 4, 1915; "Husband Jealous of Her Brothers," *Detroit Free Press*, September 26, 1916.

95 "Wife Accepts Blame," *Detroit Free Press*, June 26, 1913.

96 "Stifter Grill City's Worst, Board Told," *Toledo News-Bee*, November 15, 1917.

97 "Thieves Strip Dude to His Underwear," *Detroit Free Press,* December 3, 1916.

98 "Believe Dead Man in Street Intoxicated," *Detroit Free Press,* October 19, 1914.

99 "City Honeycombed with Gambling is Pastor's Statement," *The Windsor Evening Record,* February 17, 1913

100 "Twin Partners," *Windsor Evening Record*, July 23, 1917.

101 "Gillepsie Says He Will Crush Organized Vice," *Detroit Free Press*, August 23, 1913.

102 Doug Tracy, "Below the 'Dead Line': Toledo's Notorious Tenderloin," *The Toledo Gazette,* September 17, 2014, https://toledogazette.wordpress.com/2014/09/17/below-the-dead-line-toledos-notorious-tenderloin/.

103 "Order Rules as Vice Zone Closed," *Toledo News-Bee*, May 1, 1918.

104 "Negro Slugs and Robs Bartender in Detroit Saloon," *Detroit Free Press*, April 6, 1913; "Toughest Corners in Detroit," *Detroit Free Press*, July 6, 1913; "Beaten in Saloon on Quest for Her Husband," *Detroit Free Press*, January 14, 1913; "Spectator, Shot During Brawl in Saloon, is Dying," *Detroit Free Press,* May 27, 1915; "Constable Davis is Shot Through the Heart; Gunman is Sought as Murderer ," *Detroit Free Press,* March 8, 1916; "Skull is Fractured," *Toledo News-Bee*, April 6, 1917; "Poolroom a Crime-Breeder, Is Charge," *Toledo News-Bee*, August 6, 1917; "Armed Bandits Rob a Saloon," *TNB*, April 10, 1918.

105 "Crime Increase in Windsor for 1913 is Small," *Detroit Free Press*, February 26, 1914

106 "Rev. P.C. Cameron Urges Hearers to Forget Party," *The Windsor Evening Record*, June 22, 1914; "Pal of McIntyre Tried for Robbery," *Detroit Free Press*, January 9, 1917.

CHAPTER 4
Motoring Towards Prohibition

A prohibitionist movement had been gaining momentum in the TDW corridor since the mid-nineteenth century—well before the onslaught on regional saloons in the 1910s. In southeast Michigan, temperance and prohibition organizations rose to prominence in the 1870s and 1880s. Due to its anti-alcohol campaign, the Women's Christian Temperance Union (WCTU) quickly became the most influential dry organization in nineteenth century North America. Its ranks swelled to 150,000 members by the 1890s, which included formidable chapters in the TDW region. As Henry Ford was blazing a path for himself in the industrial world, the WCTU delivered numerous impassioned lectures about the evils of liquor in Dearborn, Detroit, and other southeastern Michigan churches. Moreover, the roots of the National Prohibition Party (NPP) can be traced directly to Detroit. John Russell, a Methodist minister from Michigan, established the first nationally-circulating prohibition newspaper in Detroit called the *Peninsular Herald*. Just a few years later, in the early 1870s, Russell became the founding chairman of the NPP. Southeastern Michigan subsequently became an early staging ground for anti-alcohol politics.[107]

Toledo and Windsor also possessed additional strong prohibitionist factions in their respective vicinities. In the late 1880s, the Glass City reportedly was home to twenty different temperance organizations. A few years later in 1893, the influential Anti-Saloon League was founded in central Ohio and quickly spread throughout the Buckeye state, including northwest Ohio. Although Toledo was a notoriously wet city, the ASL was quite active there in the early 1900s.[108] Meanwhile, Windsor's booze dealers, alcohol-serving hotels, and liquor manufacturers faced fierce opposition from the Dominion Alliance, an anti-booze network consisting of reform-minded politicians and churches.[109] During the first two decades of the twentieth centuries, Dominion Alliance representatives took to Essex County pulpits to deliver their dry messages.[110]

Anti-alcohol forces had been active in the region for decades, but it was not until the mid-1910s that dry legislation was successfully passed and implemented along the TDW corridor. Several factors contributed to the advancement of prohibitionist measures. With WWI raging in Europe, many Canadians and Americans believed the manufacture of alcohol would hamper the war effort and corrupt the young men being deployed. The precipitous rise of female political activity and voting rights quickened the pace of the dry agenda. Nativism in both Canada and the United States spurred many to view cultural drinking norms as foreign and backwards. In addition, reform-minded Progressives gained power at the local, state/provincial, and federal levels of government.

Nevertheless, it was no coincidence this happened around the same time that mass production of motor cars and a culture of automobility was permeating the area. In order to churn out cars and other related products for the growing market, local automobile magnates desired sober, timely, and diligent workers. Historian James Timberlake noted this economic argument for temperance gave the drys the "boost" they needed to advance their cause.[111]

Religious and political arguments in favor of prohibition would never be enough in an increasingly modern and industrialized American society. REO Motor Car executive Richard Scott noted that the wets could never argue against the fact "that booze never speeded up a single business, that it never made a more efficient workman."[112]

Starting in the mid-1910s, the TDW corridor's so-called "gasoline aristocracy" began to wage a dry war against the drinking establishments at their factories' gates. Earlier— before the implementation of the moving assembly line and close management of workplace processes—craft mechanics took considerable time assembling each motorcar. Whether or not laborers drank on the job or during their leisure time mattered little to supervisors; however when scale of production and efficiency became increasingly important to automobile manufacturers in the 1910s, administrators increasingly became concerned about the drinking habits of their men on the factory floor.

Gordon McGregor, the founder and president of Ford Motor Company of Canada, did

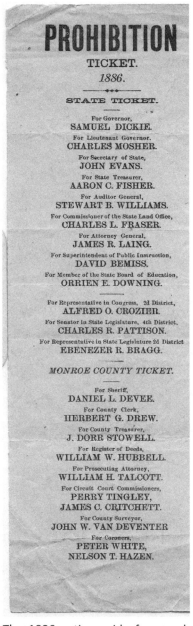

The 1886 voting guide for people supporting the "Prohibition Ticket" in Monroe County, Michigan. (Image courtesy the Monroe County Museum Archives)

everything in his power to keep a liquor-serving hotel from opening near his automobile plant in Ford City in 1913. He publicly shared gruesome stories of drunk workers injuring themselves and with racist undertones stated there would be a "serious problem" if some of his foreign employees began to drink on the job. Ultimately, McGregor and other Border Cities' automobile executives were not only able to convince local citizens to protest the new hotel but also a prominent local politician who vetoed the liquor license application.[113]

A year later in Toledo, the Overland Automobile Company boldly announced it would be opening up the world's largest cafes within its own plant.[114] Administrators hoped that this would deter its autoworkers from leaving the facility for a booze-filled lunch or dinner. Apparently, this did not have the desired effect, and a few years later a petition campaign successfully ousted the nine saloons from the neighborhoods around the Overland.[115] Even the small town of Monroe, Michigan forced out eleven bars in their factory district.[116]

Understandably, Detroit was the epicenter of a pitched battle between automobile magnates and saloonkeepers. Leading motorcar

The Ford Motor Company of Canada factory in Windsor, 1914. (Photo courtesy the Library of Congress, 2016816227)

companies such as Hudson, Packard, and others made it publicly known that they were opposed to drinking establishments plying intoxicating beverages to their employees. When an attempt was made to transfer a neighborhood liquor license to a "location directly opposite" of the Hupp Motor Company's plant on Milwaukee Avenue, the firm's president J. Walter Drake filed an appeal to the city council. "Some of our employees probably visit his saloon at noon as it is. We don't want any more attracted there through a change in location," explained Drake. "If a man drinks a beer, or any other liquor at noon it slows him up and costs the company a couple hours in efficiency." The saloonkeeper's license application was soon thereafter denied.[117]

Henry Leland, the manager of Cadillac Motor Car Company, also waged war against the bars in his factory's district. He told the *Detroit Free Press* that "manufacturers are handicapped by many things today and the saloon is among the worst detriments...There are eighteen saloons within a radius of about two blocks of our Cass avenue plant and about the same number around our other two plants. We earnestly want to see them cut out."[118] As the state prohibition referendum neared in October 1916, numerous Detroit automobile plants invited dry speakers on to their factory floors to speak directly to workers about the evils of booze. [119]

The Ford Motor Company (FMC), Henry Ford, and his team of administrators waged an early indirect war against the saloon due to their concerns about workplace efficiency. Popular memory, emphasizing the triumph of Ford's Model T and implementation of the assembly line, has shrouded early difficulties experienced on the automobile company's factory floor. The rate of producing cars was significantly hampered by what Ford supervisors had come to call the "human element." Despite the use of advanced mechanization and precise engineering of workplace ergonomics, other troubling factors like high labor turnover, soaring absenteeism, and cultural barriers prompted by the hiring of immigrant workers plagued efficient output of automobiles. Certainly, not all production issues could be attributed to employees' consumption of intoxicants, but some industrial commentators of the time claimed that drinking impacted attendance at work and overall professionalism. Moreover, when newly hired foreign-born workers, known for their strong cultural connections to alcoholic beverages, were drunk on the job it only amplified the language barrier that already hindered an efficient assembly line.[120]

Regardless of whether the alcohol problem was more perception than reality in Ford factories, Henry Ford began to demand worker sobriety not only at work but also during their leisure time, by way of official company policy.[121] In early 1914, FMC rolled out its revolutionary "Five Dollar a Day" wage, nearly double the normal pay rate of other automobile plants. Thousands of workers and immigrants flocked to the factory in Highland Park, unaware that this new wage was part of a larger paternalistic experiment by Henry Ford and his administrative team. In order to earn the full five dollars, employees had to, among other things, permit regular inspections of their houses, enroll and contribute to a savings plan, and vow to not take in boarders. These intrusive stipulations were rooted in Henry Ford's deeply held belief that a laborer's domestic life directly affected performance while they were on the clock. If Ford had direct access to an employee's lifestyle outside of the factory walls, he could then clearly discern if an employee could be relied upon inside the factory walls.[122]

It was evident Henry Ford expected his workers to abstain from drinking. A 1915 FMC pamphlet entitled "Helpful Hints and Advice to Employees" outlined the "opportunities" afforded by the company's "profit-sharing plan." At the beginning of the rules section of the pamphlet, one of the first sentences read: "Every married man, no matter what age, who can qualify as to sobriety, industry, and cleanliness, can participate."[123]

Other sources reveal the company's consternation with alcohol's impact on employees. Once in private residences, investigators' lines of questioning included or even revolved around whether workers regularly imbibed or "wasted" their earnings at the saloon. In official home investigation reports, administrators indicated whether signs of drinking were present in the household.[124] In a 1915 issue of the *Ford Times*, a FMC publication, an article entitled "The Case of Jim" pointedly singled out how consumption of booze could lead to preclusion from the company wide pay raise. In the story, an employee named Jim entered the Ford Sociological Department office and asked why he was not receiving the increased daily wage. Not only had he risen to the position

A pair of billboards in Detroit; one advertising Towar's Milk, the other, featuring an automobile, promotes Olco Whiskey. (Photo courtesy Detroit Public Library, Burton Historical Collection)

of foreman, but Jim was always "punctual and steady," as even the chief of the Sociological Bureau noted. This same administrator, nonetheless, bemoaned the negative effects of Jim's drinking, stating how Jim blew his wages at the local saloon, paying for beer and games of pool. In the eyes of the FMC, this alone justified his preclusion from the five-dollar day.[125]

Moreover, the obligation to open a savings account under the "profit-sharing plan" could be interpreted as Ford's attempt to keep his workers from local bars. As historian Madelon Powers has asserted, saloons not only provided alcoholic beverages to the laboring classes, but among other things, often served as unofficial banks where blue collar workers could cash their weekly checks. By mandating that his employees open bank accounts, Ford was further severing ties between his factory men and community drinking establishments.[126]

Word of the Ford Sociological Department's investigations filtered out through print media, spreading information about the company's strict policy against alcohol. Despite some criticism, Samuel Marquis— the Sociological Department's administrator—claimed that former employees who fought their policies were the ones "getting drunk and beating up one's wife, abusing one's family, and wasting one's money."[127]

Other newspapers and magazines were more positive about Ford's efforts, emphasizing his "untiring effort to secure sobriety" and individual success stories of reformed drunkards.[128] While other companies may have had anti-booze regulations in place before the Ford Motor Company, Henry Ford's name became known nationwide, ensuring his enmity towards intoxicants would also be widely recognized and long remembered. Ford's anti-drinking policies may have influenced other business organizations and workplaces. A journalist in 1915 reported that U.S. Steel, International Harvester, Edison, Standard Oil, and other leading firms had all just begun issuing "prompt dismissal[s]" for laborers coming to work drunk from local saloons.[129]

Not all drinking establishments, however, could be controlled by concerned automobile manufacturers or public officials. In fact, some isolated bars could attribute their existence to the rise of automobilty in the region. So-called roadhouses, which were essentially booze-serving inns or clubs situated on country roads, presented unique challenges to those who wanted to regulate or squash the liquor trade. Usually outside of city limits, urban and rural customers alike flocked to these remote watering holes because of the relative privacy these establishments offered and because they were frequently beyond the jurisdiction of municipal law enforcers. For example, the Highland Park city council and the Ford Motor Company pressed deputy sheriffs to enforce community "blue laws" upon the outlying roadhouses that were beyond the city's limits. Their pleas were ignored, and the roadhouses continued to stay open on Sundays while local deputies looked the other way.[130] In June 1915, the city council appealed to Michigan's Governor to step in. Councilman George Potts declared it was the "sworn duty" of the sheriff to take care of these roadhouses "but if they fail, then a higher power, Governor Ferris will...force the sheriff to take action or find some method to make roadhouse proprietors obey the law."[131]

Besides staying open on Sunday, TDW roadhouses faced severe criticism for a number of other reasons. For those operating outside of Windsor, reports indicated that liquor was being served to girls under the age of 18, who supposedly sought greater freedom in these isolated drinking establishments.[132] Other roadhouses located near Belle Isle on the Canadian side were frequently overrun with intoxicated Detroiters who had less respect for their surroundings. Toledo officials had been battling against roadhouses as early as 1913 when they denied eighteen liquor license applications to those planning on opening on the peripheries of the city. Issues with roadhouses began once more, however, when Toledo's Tenderloin district was cleaned up in 1918.[133] Many of these vice zone saloonkeepers simply moved their businesses outside of the city limits and beyond constant police surveillance. Rowdiness, gambling, prostitution, and illegal alcohol sales resumed in more distant locales throughout northwest Ohio's Lucas County.[134]

One infamous roadhouse was erected just across the state line in the early 1920s. The Northwood Villa, located just one mile north of the Michigan-Ohio border on the Dixie Highway, became a favored spot for drinkers, gangsters and gamblers alike.[135]

Another complaint about roadhouses coming out of Highland Park reflected a larger issue that may have contributed to the growing prohibitionist sentiment in Detroit. Highland Park officials complained about "drunken parties driving recklessly through the village" and subsequently jeopardizing the lives of residents. As more and more motorists took to the roads in the mid-1910s, and as area residents continued their drinking ways, intoxicated drivers became more prevalent.[136] One traffic safety specialist in 1915 estimated that close to half of all automobile related fatalities in Detroit were due to drivers "under the influence." Before the advent of drunk driving violations, the *Detroit Free Press* was calling for a law that ensured "these powerful machines shall be guided by drivers in complete possession of their faculties."[137]

In the years leading up to the Michigan state prohibition vote, Detroit newspaper reports detailed numerous incidents where intoxicated motorists, including professional chauffeurs, endangered the lives of pedestrians and fellow drivers.[138] In January 1916, a drunken, middle-aged man barreled through a safety zone in his "light touring car" near a busy Detroit Interurban stop. One man was killed instantly and several others severely injured. A few months later, he became the first driver in Michigan history to be convicted of vehicular manslaughter. The judge presiding over his case declared, "I give you this sentence as a warning to auto drivers who get drunk and believe they own the streets and have no regard for human life. I do this in an effort to deter reckless fools who believe that gasoline and whisky will mix." [139] Just a few days before the November 1916 prohibition vote in Michigan, the *Detroit News* published a cartoon depicting intoxicated teens with bottles in hand running over a child in their automobile. The message was clear: in the age of the automobile, consumption of booze caused havoc on the roadways.[140]

Whether or not the region's automobile culture significantly influenced the local prohibition debate in the 1910s, by mid-1919 the entire TDW corridor had become dry. In 1916, Windsor enacted prohibition as a wartime measure and then extended the legislation once the conflict ended in 1918. Detroit and the surrounding environs became dry territory in May 1918 thanks to a state prohibition referendum. Ohio would follow suit in May 1919 and notoriously wet Toledo mourned the passing of "John Barleycorn," a long-time folk personification of the

A cartoon in the January 1917 edition of *The American Issue* encouraging various states, including Ohio, to jump on the water wagon with Michigan. (Image courtesy University of Michigan, Bentley Historical Library)

alcohol trade.[141]

A region that had quickly become so enamored with automobility was now giving up one of its other beloved pastimes: drinking. However, one wet journalist pointedly questioned why drys opposed giving up their motorcars. A nationally syndicated article entitled "Shall the Automobile be Prohibited?" argued that often in fatal accidents, liquor was hastily blamed by prohibitionists and preachers as the root cause. "They never say a word about the shame and death that lurk in the automobile," countered the author. Whether or not locals grasped this supposed hypocrisy, local law enforcers likely did not fathom how the combination of dry laws and the increased presence of automobiles would make their jobs much more difficult for the next decade and a half.[142]

---

[107] Melvin Holli, *Reform in Detroit: Hazen S. Pingree and Urban Politics* (New York: Oxford University Press, 1969), 11-18; Katherine Murdock, *Domesticating Drink: Women, Men, and Alcohol in America, 1870-1940* (Baltimore: Johns Hopkins University Press, 1998), 21; Lisa Anderson, *The Politics of Prohibition: American Governance and the Prohibition Party, 1869–1933* (New York: Cambridge University Press, 2013), 70; J.R. Meador, *The Cyclopaedia of Temperance and Prohibition: A Reference Book of Facts, Statistics, and General Information on All Phases of the Drink Question, the Temperance Movement and the Prohibition Agitation* (New York: Funk & Wagnalls, 1891), 561-581.

[108] Marnie Jones, *Holy Toledo: Religion and Politics in the Life of "Golden Rule" Jones* (Lexington: University of Kentucky Press, 2015), 5, 136; "For Dry Toledo (No Joke!)," *Detroit Free Press*, April 28, 1909; "Drys Feel Out Toledo," *Detroit Free Press,* May 17, 1909.

[109] Gerald A. Hallowell, "Prohibition In Ontario, 1919-1923" Love Printing Service Ltd. Ottawa, 1972, 9; "Dry Advocates in Pulpits," *Detroit Free Press*, September 25, 1910; "Anti-Saloonists Occupy Pulpits," *Detroit Free Press,* February 12, 1912.

[110] "Temperance Fight in Essex County Planned," *Detroit Free Press*, October 26, 1913.

[111] James Timberlake, *Prohibition and the Progressive Movement* (London: Cambridge University Press, 1963), 67

[112] Larry Engelmann, *Intemperance: The Lost War Against Liquor* (New York: The Free Press, 1979), 21.

[113] David Roberts, *In the Shadow of Detroit: Gordon M. McGregor, Ford of Canada, and Motoropolis* (Detroit: Wayne State University Press, 2006), 101-103; "Charge Padding of Petition Favoring Ford City License," *The Windsor Evening Record*, April 24, 1913; "Grant Ford City License Despite Protest of Heads of Manufacturing Plants," *Windsor Evening Record,* April 25, 1913; "Would Favor Scott Act," *The Windsor Evening Record*, April 28, 1913; "Ford City to Have Two Licenses Instead of One," *Windsor Evening Record,* April 29, 1913.

[114] Overland Will Have Largest Cafe in Country," *Toledo News-Bee*, July 25, 1914.

[115] "Get Petitions to Oust Saloons Near Overland," *Toledo News-Bee,* October 23, 1916; John J. Phelan, "The Saloon as a Phase of Commercialized Amusements in Toledo," *Social Survey Series*, June 1918.

[116] "Liquor Kept Out of Monroe Shops," *Detroit Free Press,* April 14, 1914.

[117] "Factory Men Favor Lodge Saloon Plan," *Detroit Free Press*, April 21, 1914; "Business Men Favor Plan to Curb Saloons," *Detroit Free Press*, May 12, 1914.

[118] "Stop Transfer of Liquor License," *Detroit Free Press*, October 4, 1916;

[119] "Prohibition is Discussed," *Detroit Free Press*, October 4, 1916; "Prohibitionists are Busy," *Detroit Free Press,* October 5, 1916.

[120] Stephen Meyer, *The Five Dollar Day: Labor Management and Social Control in the Ford Motor Company, 1908-1921* (Albany, New York: State University of New York Press, 1981), 67-85; Ames Brown, "Nation-Wide Prohibition", The Atlantic Monthly 115 (1915): 743-748.

[121] Steven Watts, *The Peoples' Tycoon: Henry Ford and the American Century* (New York: Vintage Books, 2005) 178-182.

[122] Stephen Meyer, *The Five Dollar Day: Labor Management and Social Control in the Ford Motor Company, 1908-1921* (Albany, New York: State University of New York Press, 1981), 123-147.

[123] "New Industrial Era is Marked by Ford's Shares to Laborers," *Detroit Free Press,* January 6, 1914; "Helpful Hints and Advice to Employees: To Help Them Grasp the Opportunities which are Presented to Them by the Ford Profit-Sharing Plan" Ford Motor Company, 1915.

[124] John Fitch, "Ford of Detroit and His Ten Million Dollar Profit Sharing Plan", *The Survey*, vol. 31, 1915, 547; Boris Emmet, Profit Sharing in the United States (Washington: Government Printing Office, 1917) 99-100.

[125] Kirk Alexander, "The Case of Jim," *Ford Times* vol. 8, 1915, 69-70.

[126] Madelon Powers, *Faces Along the Bar: Lore and Order in the Workingman's Saloon,* 1870-1920 (Chicago: University of Chicago Press, 1998), 67-68; "Police Arrest 50 in Gambling Raids," *Detroit Free Press*, February 14, 1916; "Peace Plan Goes Into Ford Homes," *Detroit Free Press*, March 15, 1916.

[127] "Ford, in Helping Cancer Victims, Asks Aid of You," *Toledo News Bee*, July 2, 1914; "Modern Warfare Against the Saloon," *Perrysburg Journal*, November 9, 1916; The Ford Plan for Employees' Betterment", *The Iron Age* vol. 93, 1914, 306-309; John Fitch, "Ford of Detroit and His Ten Million Dollar Profit Sharing Plan", *The Survey*, vol. 31, 1915, 547; Boris Emmet, Profit Sharing in the United States (Washington: Government Printing Office, 1917) 99-100; Samuel Marquis, *Henry Ford: An Interpretation* (Detroit, Michigan: Wayne State University Press, 2007), 98-99.

[128] John R. Lee, "The So-Called Profit Sharing System in the Ford Plant," *Annals of the American Academy of Political and Social Science*, Vols. 63-65, 297-310.

[129] Ida Tarbell, *New Ideals in Business: An Account of Their Practice and Their Effects Upon Men and Profits* (New York: MacMillion, 1916), 127-129; L. Ames Brown, "Nationwide Prohibition", *The Atlantic Monthly* vol. 115, 1915, 743.

[130] "May Invoke Ferris for Sunday "Lid", *Detroit Free Press*, June 3, 1915.

[131] "Roadhouses Are to be Prosecuted in Highland Park," *Detroit Free Press*, July 21, 1915; "Police Arrest 50 in Gambling Raids," *Detroit Free Press,* February 14, 1916.

[132] "To Protect Young Girls," *Detroit Free Press,* July 5, 1914.

[133] "Pine Creek Hotel Refused License," *Detroit Free Press,* April 23, 1915; "Toledo Board is Adding to Record of Tough Saloons," *Detroit Free Press*, November 16, 1913.

134 "Police Report Many Women Leaving City," *Toledo News-Bee*, March 25, 1918; "Brewer Gave Tip In Raid On 'Leggers," *Toledo News-Bee*, August 1, 1917. "Order Rules as Toledo's Vice Zone Closed," May 1, 1918, *Toledo News-Bee*; "Adams-St House is Raided by Police" *Toledo News-Bee*, May 6, 1918; "Arrest Scores in Sunday Raid on Roadhouse", *Toledo News-Bee*, May 6, 1918.

135 "Hayes' Villa is Raided," *Toledo News-Bee*, August 24, 1924

136 "May Invoke Ferris for Sunday 'Lid'," *Detroit Free Press*, June 3, 1915; "Safety Advocate Blames Deaths on Drunken Autoists," *Detroit Free Press*, October 8, 1915; "Highland Park Still Wars on Auto Speeder," *Detroit Free Press*, August 21, 1913.

137 "No Place for Drunken Men," *Detroit Free Press*, October 28, 1914 "Wild Car Ride Ends in Death," *Detroit Free Press*, September 20, 1917; "Auto Hurls Death Into Group in Safety Zone; Policeman Stops Escape," *Detroit Free Press*, January 10, 1916.

138 "Reckless Driving in Charged Chauffeur," *Detroit Free Press*, November 2, 1914;

139 "Auto Strikes Three Sisters at Corner; One Dead, Two Hurt," *Detroit Free Press*, October 27, 1914.

140 Larry Engelmann, "O, Whisky: The History of Prohibition in Michigan," Dissertation, University of Michigan, 1971, 288-290.

141 Ibid.

142 "Shall the Automobile be Prohibited," *The Wine and Spirit Bulletin*, vol. 30, 1916, 67.

CHAPTER 5
Test Drive #1: Early Dry Enforcement in the Canadian Border Cities, 1916-1919

In the days leading up to September 16, 1916, many "hotelmen" and innkeepers in Canadian border cities were getting anxious. With the Ontario Temperance Act scheduled to take effect at 7:00 p.m. that Saturday night, they still had sizeable stocks of beer and liquor. Luckily for them, business picked up as the start of dry enforcement approached, so much so that many locations selling alcohol could be easily identified by the long lines wrapping around the buildings, "similar to that at any popular movie theater."[143]

The *Detroit Free Press* lampooned some of the "wild scenes" that ensued in downtown Windsor during the last few wet hours. The counters of hotel saloons and wholesale liquor dealers were jam-packed, "lined five and six deep," and among the throngs were mothers who brought their children along with them to purchase booze. One elderly woman—apparently desperate and poor as well—"went to her knees and prayed to the clerk to give her a supply of liquor free of charge," only to be discharged with tears streaming from her eyes. Out on the streets, a large boisterous crowd sang "How Dry I Am" while heckling a competing parade of temperance advocates. Mob mentality ultimately took hold as liquor and champagne bottles were stolen and many imbibers had to be ejected from hotel barrooms.[144]

Beyond these peculiar vignettes of human behavior, the increasing popularity of the automobile was evident on September 16 and during the earliest dry days in the Border Cities area. Rural farmers drove into downtown Windsor to legally purchase booze one last time, carrying away "every kind of receptacle filled with liquor ranging from gasoline cans to medicine bottles." Once the clock struck 7:00 p.m., some Windsorites who were still thirsty took the ferry dock across the Detroit River into wet territory. Drunken pedestrians were quickly rounded up and directed by Detroit's officers to take the next ferry back. Those who decided to take their personal vehicles, however, were able to "dig themselves in" along Woodward Avenue. Upon returning to the ferry dock in a "zigzagging" manner, many intoxicated automobilists fell easily into a police trap. By the end of the night, the Detroit Police Department's well-known "big black cars" had delivered numerous tipsy Canadians to the central police station.[145]

A few weeks later, on October 4, 1916, customs officials posted at the Windsor and Walkerville ferries were ordered to be "more particular in searching autos and persons suspected of smuggling" liquor across the Detroit River into Canada. Less than a week later, 200 quarts of liquor had been confiscated. While some people had been caught with liquor in their vehicles, according to newspaper reports the majority of those arrested with alcohol were hiding it in their clothes. All of the violators were first-time offenders and were subsequently released without charges.[146]

From 1916 to 1919 automobiles became accessories in liquor law violations around the Border Cities area, a series of towns and communities, such as Windsor, on the Canadian side of the Detroit River. A loophole in the Ontario Temperance Act (OTA) allowed Canadian residents to import alcohol and Canadian businesses to manufacture alcohol.[147] Residents in Ontario would place an order with a licensed liquor dealer in Detroit. An automobile deliveryman working for the

Detroit dealer would pick up the requested liquor from a local Canadian distillery – such as Hiram Walker's in Walkerville – and "import" it to the Windsor-area residence.[148] Since the order was placed in Detroit, the entire transaction was legal. Often, these Detroit-based liquor importation offices would openly advertise in Essex County newspapers, bragging about their same day delivery and 24-hour service. Such deliveries became illegal in March 1918 when the Canadian government made it illegal during wartime to import alcohol into provinces that had banned sale of alcoholic beverages.[149]

Liquor law violators were rarely caught in their automobiles because the Windsor Police Department lacked the resources to aggressively go after smugglers on wheels. In 1917 the Windsor police only possessed two motorcycles and one outdated, chain drive patrol wagon, which

A brewery truck loads up at a Canadian warehouse, across the river from Detroit, ca 1925. (Photo courtesy the *Detroit News*)

was almost exclusively used to transport those arrested and as an ambulance in medical emergencies. Across the river, by 1912 the Detroit Police Department had fourteen motorcycles and several cars for its "flying squadron," a division that specialized in responding to crimes in progress.[150] In contrast, if a rumrunner in an automobile sneaked past the customs officials at the Canadian riverfront, it was unlikely local police would pursue them.

The few automobilized rumrunners caught in the Border Cities area during this time period, were typically arrested at the ferry docks or implicated in stealing alcoholic cargo from freight trains traveling through. One of these rare instances occurred on August 22, 1918, when a "fair liquor smuggler" from Detroit attempted to sneak six pints of whiskey and a quart of liquor past custom officials working at the Walkerville ferry. Unfortunately, for her, one of the bottles hidden in the back seat of her vehicle spilled on the upholstery and the officer detected its smell. The Detroit woman paid $205 in fines.[151] Border Cities' newspaper reports in 1918 also document a wave of booze thieves targeting trains. In one instance, a witness admitted to unloading crates of stolen Scotch whiskey from train cars into several automobiles.[152]

Analyzing the earliest prohibition period on the TDW corridor— which has largely been ignored by historians—provides greater context to the Volstead era in the region. Even before the United States went dry in 1920, the greater Windsor era was essentially allowing individuals transporting alcohol in automobiles to operate freely in Canadian territory. Moreover, Americans and Canadians were already developing business relationships that exploited the weaknesses in prohibition laws in borderland regions. Motor vehicles were becoming essential tools in rumrunning culture. This would especially hold true along the Michigan-Ohio state line starting on May 1, 1918, when the Wolverine state's dry law took effect.

Canadians and Americans alike were fascinated with how Detroit and its citizenry would react to state prohibition. Michigan's dry law meant the Motor City's 1,250 saloons and sixteen breweries would suddenly be closed and an estimated 9,000 employees in local alcohol industries would lose their jobs. As the *Amherstburg Echo* succinctly put it, "Detroit's behavior would be watched throughout the United States." The Anti-Saloon League rejoiced in the fact that the Motor City would "soon be the largest Prohibition city in the nation if not the world." Perhaps interested parties should have focused their attention a little more to the south, where Monroe County dry enforcers would wage a year-long battle with automobilized smugglers crossing over from wet northwest Ohio.[153]

---

[143] "Residents of Border Towns Lay in Liquor," *Detroit Free Press,* September 16, 1916.

[144] "Wild Scenes in Windsor as Lids Falls on Bars," *Detroit Free Press*, September 17, 1916.

[145] "Police of Detroit Cooperate with Windsor Authorities in Enforcing Prohibition Orders," *The Windsor Evening Record,* September 18, 1916; "Wild Scenes in Windsor as Lids Falls on Bars," *Detroit Free Press*, September 17, 1916.

[146] "Close Watch of Smugglers of 'Wet Goods' Here," *The Windsor Evening News Record*, October 4, 1916; "Smugglers Loose 200 Qts. of Liquor Here," *Detroit Free Press*, October 11, 1916.

[147] "Dry Ontario by Fall is Certain," *Detroit Free Press*, March 26, 1916.

[148] "Can Deliver Beer from Warehouse," *Detroit Free Press*, September 21, 1916.

[149] "Will Bring Liquor Agents to Court," *Detroit Free Press*, April 11, 1917 "Tighter Liquor Lid on Essex Planned," *Detroit Free Press*, December 29, 1917; "Quick Service — One Day Delivery!" *Windsor Evening Record*, May 22, 1917; "United Liquor Co." *Windsor Evening Record*, December 29,1917; Patrick Brode, *Dying for a Drink: How a Prohibition Preacher Got Away with Murder* (Biblioasis: Windsor, Ontario, 2018), 18. Close analysis of area newspapers during this time period only revealed a few instances of cars being used in crimes involving alcohol. One instance occurred when a group of railroad employees organized to steal crates of scotch from a rail car. They used an automobile to transport and hide the alcoholic cache. See "Scotch is Buried; Stolen by Thieves," *Detroit Free Press,* August 18, 1918.

[150] C.H. Gervais, *The Border Police: One Hundred and Twenty-Five Years of Policing in Windsor* (Penumbra Press: Newcastle, Ontario, 1992) "How the Police, Fire, Water, Lighting, and Other Public Service Departments Have Advanced in Keeping with Other Lines," *Detroit Free Press*, November 10, 1912.

[151] "Fair Liquor Smuggler Draws Down $205 Fine," *Border Cities' Star*, August 22, 1918.

[152] "Whiskey Thief is Sentenced to 18 Months," *Border Cities' Star*, September 5, 1918; "Freed on Liquor Theft Charges," *Border Cities' Star,* September 12, 1918; "Even Camoflaged Whiskey Tickles Palates of Many," *Border Cities' Star*, August 13, 1918;

[153] "Town and County," *Amherstberg Echo,* April 26, 1918; "A Word of Greeting from the Associate State Superintendent," *The American Issue*, Michigan edition, March 1918.

CHAPTER 6
A Porous Border: State Prohibition's Early Effects on Southeast Michigan and Northwest Ohio

In the early morning hours of February 7, 1919, troopers from the Michigan State Constabulary shook off the bitter winter cold and set their sights southward towards the Ohio border. From their position just south of Monroe, the officers had been given the difficult job of halting rum-running gangs that would whiz by in their powerful automobiles with reckless abandon. Just after 3:00 a.m. they spotted the headlights of a caravan of approaching cars, that were likely jammed full of illegal booze.

Sure enough, the first car sped by, refusing orders to stop. Squad No. 1 signaled to the other set of policemen, who were waiting further along the road. Message received, Squad No. 2 plopped a telephone pole across the roadway. At 70 miles an hour, the vehicle "struck the barrier," bounded into the air, and hurled the passengers and bottles of whiskey "out like peas." As the newspaper reported later that day, the automobile "turned turtle" and completely wrecked. Two occupants of the car—both Toledoans—were knocked unconscious but miraculously suffered just minor injuries. However, both smugglers interestingly claimed a third man, "Eddy," was driving the vehicle and did not end up in the County jail with them. Despite the sheriff department's denial, unfounded but "persistent rumors" flooded Monroe that local enforcement officials had covered up the potentially controversial death of a booze runner. Immediately word of this new "rumstopper" spread within Toledo's saloon culture, where signs openly offered a handsome monetary reward for the deaths of the officers who partook in the incident.[154]

C.B. Southworth, the mayor of Monroe, seized the opportunity to voice his long-held frustrations with prohibition enforcement in and around his city. "Instead of firing guns and putting logs across the roads, the state should install toll gates and quietly, without all this wild west show, stop the whisky runners," Southworth told a *Toledo Blade* reporter.[155] He even penned an open letter to Michigan Governor Albert Sleeper that was published in the *Detroit Free Press*. Southworth wrote, "Can you give me any good reason why your state police taking Wayne County whisky tolls off at Monroe instead of in Wayne County?" The mayor concluded that many within his community were "getting tired of Detroit and Wayne County slush being dumped off at Monroe." Government officials in Lansing, upset with all of the controversy, ordered the troopers involved in the log incident to never repeat it again.[156]

As exemplified by this incident, rumrunners' use of automobiles further complicated officers' attempts to enforce dry laws along the TDW corridor. Historians have detailed how dry agents during the Volstead Era (1920 to 1933) strong-armed suspects, accepted bribes, and engaged in many other controversial policing tactics. However, scholars have largely overlooked the seminal role motorcars played in rumrunning culture and the unique predicaments this presented to prohibition enforcers.[157]

With Ontario first succumbing to wartime prohibition in 1916, Michigan following suit in 1918, and Ohio finally in 1919, state, provincial, and national borders were supposed to be firm boundaries that clearly demarcated dry and wet territory. The widespread presence of automobiles and their use in illegal smuggling would challenge the nature of these borderlands.

Also neglected by prohibition historians is that when the Eighteenth Amendment became law in 1920, policemen throughout the TDW corridor already had plenty of experience fighting an unceasing tide

LOG TRAP WRECKED THIS BOOZE CAR

Overturned car and smashed bottles show what the Michigan state police did to one rum runner near Monroe Friday.

Cyril Grude, Toledo, and his brother, occupants of the car, carrying 400 quarts of liquor, were slightly hurt and are now in jail at Monroe, charged with rum smuggling.

The driver attempted to speed through the guards, but was caught by a log trap further up the road.

In February 1919 a pair of brothers from Toledo escaped serious injury when their car collided with a log at 70 miles per hour near Monroe. The log had been laid across the road by Michigan State Constabulary in an effort to stop the suspected rumrunners. More than 400 quarts of liquor were found amid the wreckage.

of rumrunners and alcohol-related crimes. Between 1916 and 1919, the region became nationally known for its problems in stemming the illegal liquor trade. Closer analysis of this brief period not only reveals problems that would plague the Volstead era, but also the difficulties of being a dry agent during the Age of the Automobile.

Michigan's first dry day was easier than expected for Monroe County officials. The only liquor law violator arrested was a transient railroad employee who offered the sheriff an intoxicating beverage. The only other incidents happened on Dixie Highway, the north-south route that cut through the county and saw an ever-increasing number of automobiles travelling between Toledo and Detroit. Nevertheless, the unpaved portions of the Dixie frequently became a notorious mud pit during the wet spring months. It was not a surprise when the *Monroe Evening News* reported that two Detroit trucks attempting to relocate booze to Toledo—which was still wet territory—remained stuck on the highway on May 1. Instead of arresting the drivers and confiscating their alcoholic cargo as required by law, local deputies ordered the loads hauled south of the Michigan state line as soon as the trucks made their way out of their muddy ruts.[158]

Ironically, this enforcement decision was perhaps one of the easiest made during the first full dry year in Monroe County, Michigan. The efforts of local officers to police the illegal transporting of booze through their jurisdiction were hampered, especially when rumrunners utilized motor vehicles. As the culture of automobility was booming around them, regional law enforcers had to make hasty decisions about which motorists to stop and search and what to do when they did not stop. In turn, heated confrontations along Monroe County roadways increased public concern over aggressive policing, especially for those behind the wheel. For smugglers violating the dry laws with the aid of cars, the culture of automobility enabled incredible success and profits. These developments were particularly acute in Monroe County, where a so-called "Great Booze Rush" would make enforcement of Michigan's state prohibition law a daunting task.

Even before the dry law took effect on May 1, 1918, Monroe County officials were concerned with how state prohibition would impact traffic on the Dixie Highway. By the time state prohibition had run its course, this heavily traveled two-lane road earned two fitting nicknames: the "Avenue de Booze" and the "Rummers' Runway."[159]

Local officials were justifiably worried about the "thirsty of Detroit" who traveled to and from Toledo for a night of legal drinking. They warned motorists "they had better have their gas tanks overflowing [rather] than themselves." To demonstrate how serious they were about reckless and drunk driving, deputies took "drastic action" during the month of April 1918, fining any driver that exceeded the 30 mile per hour speed limit.[160] Dozens of complaints about the officers patrolling the Dixie were being filed with the Detroit Automobile Club (DAC). The DAC and Toledo Automobile Club ultimately agreed with the conduct of law enforcement in Monroe County, with the DAC stating that all "parties concerned should endeavor to assist in the regulation of traffic so that the main highway between Detroit and Toledo can be safe for all drivers." The *Monroe Evening News* also noted that conditions on the Dixie would likely worsen if "some of the Michigan pilgrims carry back excess cargoes from the Buckeye state."[161] Strict enforcement on the roadways before prohibition, it was believed, would decrease enforcement issues during the upcoming dry days.

These warnings and enforcement practices appear to have worked during the first weeks of state prohibition in Michigan. Very few motorists were arrested early on for drunk driving or rumrunning on Monroe County roads. The vast majority of those violating the liquor laws in May and June were caught on the regional Interurban, an electric trolley system that connected Detroit, Toledo, and points in between. A total of 64 smugglers and drunks were arrested on Monroe County trolleys during the first full dry month, in comparison to just nine rumrunning motorists. In an attempt to avoid officers hawking the Dixie, men and women from Michigan routinely took the Interurban down to the nearby oasis of Toledo to engage in a night of unbridled intoxication. Toledo arrest records and newspaper accounts document how Michiganders converged upon the city in droves, and that many did not leave without a stay in the city jail and a fine. On July 4, 1918, 108 of the 156 people arrested in downtown Toledo hailed from Michigan and the vast majority of Michiganders were jailed for a drunk and disorderly charge.[162] *The National Police Journal* noted that Toledo's police blotters resembled "a Detroit City directory" since the Wolverine State went dry.[163]

Other northwestern Ohio locales were also feeling the effects of Michigan's prohibition law. Washington Township, sandwiched between Toledo and the state line, contained several small hamlets, rural areas, and lakeside communities, of which Point Place was the fastest-growing. A northern Toledo suburb situated along the confluence of the Ottawa River and Lake Erie, Point Place in the late 1910s had attracted "scores of families" seeking "open space and naturally pleasant surroundings." Permanent homes quickly replaced the "flimsy" summer cottages that used to dot the lakeshore. However, once the alcohol ban took effect just across the border in early May 1918, intense debate over the "liquor traffic" divided area residents. Devoted drys in Washington Township attempted to exploit the TDW region's automobility culture in their attempts to drive saloons out of the township. "The joy parties from Detroit and other Michigan towns now dry will hit the Washington township saloons first," warned one concerned local who favored an eradication of all nearby drinking establishments. "It won't be safe to drive an automobile on the Point Place road and approaches to other saloons this summer unless they are voted out."[164]

Soon a petition was circulating with the intention of spurring a special election to make Washington Township dry. H.H. Bassett, a local proponent of the petition, bemoaned what was already occurring in Point Place. He told the *Toledo Blade* that upon asking for signatures, it was discovered that fourteen "underworld women" from Toledo's old Tenderloin district were now residing at Point Place. Bassett continued, "Out of nine automobiles that stopped at a place in Point Place, seven had Michigan licenses. That is indication already of what we will have if the saloon goes in at Point Place." The notion of automobilized Michigan drinkers flooding the area was apparently frightening enough that by the first week of May they had gathered enough signatures to forcing a special election on July 2.[165]

In the month and half leading up to the special election, Point Place became a frequent subject of scrutiny. A well-publicized police raid on the edge of town in the early morning hours of May 19 seemed to prove that Michiganders were more than happy to drive to obscure locations just outside of Toledo for a drink. Tipped off by the dozens of automobiles parked outside, officers identified two "roadhouses" diagonally across the street from each other and entered the establishments with guns drawn. Upon the cops' surprise entry, inebriated men and women scurried towards the closest exits and some even jumped out of second floor windows to avoid capture.[166] Police on the scene estimated that 200 drinkers had successfully escaped on foot, leaving their parked cars behind. A local newspaper also shared that "300 motorists drove up and turned away when they found the police there." Still, the haul was quite impressive: 87 men and women—comprised mostly of young men from Michigan, local prostitutes, and illegal liquor dealers—and several car loads of whiskey, beer, and wine. Among the arrested were twenty Detroiters, "said to be the sons of prominent men," and the roadhouses' owners. One of these proprietors happened to be Charles Kennedy, uncle and mentor of future bootlegging martyr and Toledo legend Jack Kennedy.[167]

Over a month later, as the Washington Township dry election neared, the *Toledo Blade* ran a front-page article entitled "Resorts Run Wide Open at Point Place." According to the newspaper, the number of prostitutes operating at Point Place grew from fourteen to 100 in less than two months. With a "discordant serenade" of electric pianos playing in the background, these disorderly resorts also sold liquor openly and provided illegal gambling games to its visitors. Once again, it was emphasized that out-of-state "motor parties" were the "principal frequenters of the district." Local residents complained to the Toledo Police Department, but it was to no avail; Point Place fell under the Lucas County Sheriff's jurisdiction and he seemingly had little interest in cleaning out the lakeside community.

The *Toledo Blade* made its dry position clearly known in its editorial page a week later. Not just condemning the state of moral decay in Point Place, the newspaper claimed that allowing legal drinking establishments to increase in the area was equivalent to "applying a match to tinder." *The Blade* also employed the language of automobility to encourage Washington Township residents to vote out the saloon. The township, the newspaper argued, had become a "veritable No Man's Land," where "excursionists" from north of the state line could engage in "surreptitious drinking" without worrying about Toledo city police or Michigan dry agent enforcement. *The Blade* warned, "It is no figure of speech to say that its roads will become avenues of danger, its peace and quiet shattered, and itself a harborage for unbridled drinking parties."[168]

The editorial did not have the desired effect. On July 2, Washington Township residents voted 638 to 566 to remain wet. The number of legal saloons in the township would increase, their proprietors hoping to profit from the swarms of thirsty Michiganders expected in Ohio. V.A. Schreiber, who headed the local branch of the Toledo Anti-Saloon League, attributed the defeat to a large contingent of "male parasites" who had recently settled in Point Place with "red light district" women.

According to Schreiber, the men had moved into the community by May 1, so they met the 60-day residency requirement – by just a few days – and were eligible to vote on July 2.[169]

---

[154] Rumored One Has Been Killed," *Monroe Evening News*, February 7, 1919; Frank B. Elser "Keeping Detroit on the Water Wagon," *Outlook*, 121 (April 2, 1919), 561; Larry Engelmann, "Booze: The Ohio Connection, 1918-1919," *Detroit in Perspective: A Journal of Regional History*, 2 (Winter 1975), 123.

[155] "Police Ordered to Give Constabulary No Help in Apprehending Liquor Violators," *The Toledo Blade*, February 8, 1919.

[156] "Monroe Protests Wayne Gin Running," *Detroit Free Press*, February 11, 1919; Frank B. Elser "Keeping Detroit on the Water Wagon," *Outlook*, 121 (April 2, 1919), 561; Larry Engelmann, "Booze: The Ohio Connection, 1918-1919," *Detroit in Perspective: A Journal of Regional History*, 2 (Winter 1975), 123.

[157] See Charles Merz, *The Dry Decade* (New York City: Doubleday, 1931), Andrew Sinclair, *Prohibition, The Era of Excess. With a Pref. by Richard Hofstadter* (Boston: Little, Brown, 1962), Larry Engelmann, *Intemperance: The Lost War Against Liquor* (New York: Free Press, 1979), Edward Behr, *Prohibition: Thirteen Years That Changed America* (New York: Arcade Pub., 1996), Daniel Okrent, *Last Call: The Rise and Fall of Prohibition, 1920-1933* (New York: Scribner, 2010) and Lisa McGirr, *The War on Alcohol: Prohibition and the Rise of the American State* (New York City: W.W. Norton &, 2016). The only Prohibition studies to explicitly connect the period of Prohibition to automobile culture are W. J. Rorabaugh, *Prohibition: A Concise History* (Oxford University Press, 2018) and Neal Thompson, *Driving with the Devil: Southern Moonshine, Detroit Wheels, and the Birth of Nascar* (New York: Three Rivers Press, 2007). Rorabaugh only devotes a few pages to analyzing the automobiles role during the Prohibition period. Thompson focuses primarily on how rum-runners' use of cars in the South led ultimately to the development of stock car racing.

[158] "Saloons Quietly Closed Tuesday; No Disturbances," *Monroe Evening News*, May 1, 1918.

[159] "Michigan's 'Great Booze Rush' and its Suppression by State and Federal Action," *Literary Digest* vol. 60, March 15, 1919, 85-86.

[160] "Imbibers Better Stay Off Monroe Toledo Highway," *Monroe Evening News*, April 30, 1918.

[161] Ibid.

[162] "Register of Arrests: From July 1, 1918 to September 5, 1918," Central Station: City of Toledo, Toledo Police Department Safety Building Attic, Book 39, 18-32.

[163] "Toledo's Reorganized Police Force," *The National Police Journal*, March 1919, 3-5.

[164] "Open Fight on Township Bars," *Toledo Blade*, May 4, 1918; "Editorial," *Toledo Blade*, July 1, 1918.

[165] "Drys Obtain Many Names on Petition," *Toledo Blade*, May 6, 1918.

[166] "Girls, Trapped by Police, Leap Far", *Toledo News-Bee*, May 20, 1918.

[167] "Police Arrest Nearly Hundred", *Toledo Blade*, May 20, 1918; Kenneth R. Dickson, "...Nothing Personal, Just Business...": Prohibition and Murder on Toledo's Mean Streets* (Fremont, OH: Lesher Printing, 2006), 50.

[168] "Resorts Run Wide Open at Point Place," *Toledo Blade*, June 26, 1918; "Editorial," *Toledo Blade*, July 1, 1918.

[169] "Township Votes Wet, Number of Saloons May Be Increased," *Toledo Blade*, July 3, 1918.

CHAPTER 7
Test Drive #2: Early Dry Enforcement in Monroe County, Michigan

While Toledo and Point Place dealt with an influx of drinking Michiganders, as the summer of 1918 progressed, law enforcement officials in Monroe County confronted more and more motorists attempting to sneak booze back across the border. At first, only a handful of deputy sheriffs were actively patrolling roadways for liquor violators in automobiles. An incident near the state line, in the small town of Erie, Michigan, would transform the nature of policing prohibition in the region. On the morning of June 20, an ex-saloonkeeper, a bartender, and a Detroit policeman were speeding home in a taxicab after a night of carousing in Toledo. Due to its high rate of speed as it passed through the small village, the taxi was pulled over by an officer stationed there. The drunken bartender opted to throw his beer bottle out his passenger window, perhaps in an attempt to get rid of incriminating evidence. Just as the bottle was thrown, a military convoy of trucks were heading south on the Dixie. The bottle hit one of the soldier-drivers just above the eye, "inflicting two deep cuts." The soldier was rushed to Flower Hospital, just across the state line in Sylvania, Ohio. A day later, the bartender was accused of aiming the bottle at the military truck and was given the largest prohibition fine up to that point.[170]

After receiving word of the beer bottle incident in Erie, Michigan

81

Governor Albert Sleeper called for an emergency conference in Monroe. Discussing how to stop the "rough acts" being perpetrated on the county's roads, local officials, the State Dairy and Food Commissioner of Michigan, and Colonel Roy C. Vandercook of the Michigan State Constabulary ultimately decided that "radical measures" were needed. It was decided that 24 mounted troopers from the State Constabulary— the predecessor to the Michigan State Police—would be deployed to the Michigan-Ohio border to halt drivers suspected of intoxication or transporting alcohol. Explicitly mentioning the beer bottle incident, the *Monroe Evening News* confidently asserted that this decision would "undoubtedly put an end to the rowdyism."[171]

Arriving on horseback on the afternoon of June 27, 1918, the "khaki clad" Michigan State troopers were welcomed with "quite an amount of excitement" in downtown Monroe. Colonel Vandercook and his troopers then rode south towards the state line, fittingly setting up camp in the small town of Temperance, just four miles west of Erie. The local newspaper announced that the Constabulary would be stationed on every north-south road running through Monroe County to confront the automobile rumrunners head on. Expecting some difficulties at first, Colonel Vandercook also issued a statement: "We ask Monroe people to be patient at first, at any little inconvenience which may be caused."[172]

The first few weeks of prohibition enforcement were a tremendous success for the Michigan State Constabulary. They not only arrested 40 motorists and passengers for violating the state's dry laws during their first weekend of duty, but they also seemed to be establishing a rapport with law-abiding locals. A *Monroe Evening News* reporter tagged along with the State troopers for one of the first days of enforcement as regional tourists simultaneously headed for the beach resorts that used to dot the Monroe County lakeshore. He noted that for a two-hour period the Constabulary's men stopped, questioned, and searched "over 100 machines" just south of Erie. Despite troopers causing lengthy back-ups on the right hand side of the Dixie, many of those who were stopped reportedly took "the situation good naturedly" and joked with the police. One of the automobiles halted contained "several well-known young society ladies" from Monroe and no booze, but instead of spurring anxiety or anger, the search "caused much amusement" for the women. In another vehicle, the mounted Constabulary found four Toledo nurses who would soon leave the country to tend to wounded and sick doughboys in Europe. The females playfully offered their pet poodle to the officers. Further demonstrating the local curiosity with the new dry enforcers, it was reported that "a large number of Monroe people motored to Temperance to see the camp and watch the men searching the machines."[173]

The troopers quickly discovered that rumrunners were utilizing the region's culture of automobility to shroud their illegal activities. The first booze smuggler to be caught by the Constabulary was a well-known Detroit grocer returning from Toledo in his company truck. It was not unusual for grocerymen or other business owners to traverse

Colonel Roy C. Vandercook of the Michigan State Constabulary. (Image courtesy University of Michigan, Bentley Historical Library)

the Dixie Highway to transport foodstuffs and goods from Toledo. It was, however, peculiar that baskets of vegetables "clinked considerably" when the Constabulary searched the vehicle. Within what seemed to be "a nice basket of sweet corn" was actually a "small brewery," reported the local newspaper. After removing the top layer of produce, the dry agents uncovered fourteen quarts of beer, one gallon of whiskey, three pints of gin, and one quart of wine.[174]

The grocer also happened to have his wife alongside him in the truck, perhaps hoping that a female passenger would avert suspicion and a thorough search. Despite the fact that women were increasingly getting behind the wheel in the late 1910s and 1920s, it was much more common to perceive females as non-criminal travelers going to picnics, local tourist sites, or simply "joy-riding" with their significant others, family, or a group of friends. This tactic of bringing along a lady in rumrunning endeavors was thought to provide a proverbial veil of innocence and would be utilized by professional smugglers for the next decade and a half. Nevertheless, exploiting this feminine aspect of automobility did not always work for those secretly transporting illegal alcohol. Just a few days after the arrest of the Detroit grocer, two hotel proprietors from Wyandotte were driving back from Toledo with their wives, attempting to give the outward impression of a wholesome outing in the Glass City. Pulled over by the Constabulary, a handbag revealed a small cache of beer and whiskey. The men were hauled off to the Monroe jail and the women were allowed to drive the rumrunning vehicle back to Wyandotte.[175]

All of the officers in Monroe County involved in enforcing the state's dry law were being commended for their rigorous efforts. Two weeks after the Constabulary's arrival, the *Monroe Evening News* reported "arrests in the last few days have been dwindling." In fact, on July 15, the police arrested just five bootleggers, the smallest numbers since the state went dry. Lansing was pleased with the results, too. Governor Sleeper penned a letter to the local dry agents, commending the good policing work in Monroe and assured that his office "will stand behind you in every particular, to see that the statute will be enforced."[176]

Emboldened by this full-fledged support, area agents noticeably became more aggressive in their policing of the liquor law as the summer progressed. Reports of officers aiming and shooting their revolvers at vehicles suspected of rumrunning appeared for the first time in local newspapers. Moreover, in mid-September the Michigan State Constabulary did the unthinkable when they apprehended two prominent Monroe men for smuggling booze in their automobile. Journalists claimed that these arrests demonstrated that the troopers no longer had any "regard for anyone's feeling or station in life." The state authorities also started to engage in very "thorough inspections" of cars and even started to confiscate the vehicles of rumrunners. Collectively, these bold actions not only stirred up controversies over private property and the rights of motorists, but they also caused some Monroe County residents to reconsider their positive perception of local law enforcers.[177]

Two prohibition enforcement incidents in the fall of 1918 garnered significant attention for the Michigan State Constabulary and other liquor agents in the area. On September 29, state troopers and investigators surrounded and captured the Billingsley gang, perhaps the most infamous rum-running ring in the country at the time. The gang, consisting of several brothers and their accomplices, had previously operated a criminal organization in other dry states like Oklahoma and Washington. However, once Michigan voted dry, the gang planned to move its base of operations to the TDW corridor. The region promised to be a profitable prohibition paradise when Detroit became the largest city in the United States to "get on the water wagon." The Billingsleys quickly purchased a Toledo warehouse, a fleet of vehicles, large stocks of wholesale Ohio liquor and several small Detroit grocery stores. They would then transport their alcoholic cargo by truck from Toledo north through Monroe County and then distribute the illegal supply to a variety of Detroit restaurants and speakeasies from their shops.[178]

On the night of their capture, the gang was attempting to move over 1,500 quarts of booze from Toledo to Detroit in a "cavalcade" of cars and trucks. They were lured into an isolated spot near Lambertville, Michigan by a young private investigator named William Chase who had been infiltrating the group for weeks. Chase first discovered the Billingsley operation when working in Detroit and noticing the exorbitant number of vehicles stopping at one of their small grocery stores. He quickly gained the gang's trust, assisting them as load after load of booze was motored across the state line and north on Michigan roadways. While Michigan's dry agents were waiting for the right opportunity to surprise the rumrunners, Chase was keeping track of their liquor sales. In just over a month, the Billingsleys had smuggled over $160,000 worth of booze into Detroit.[179]

Once in custody, the officers confiscated the five vehicles and used

In September 1918 the Michigan State Constabulary busted a caravan of cars operated by the Billingsley gang. Stopping the crew near Lambertville, Michigan, the cops seized 1,500 quarts of liquor. (Photo courtesy Michigan State University).

them to transport the smugglers separately. Captain Charles Koch steered one of the cars with the gang's mastermind, Sherman Billingsley, handcuffed in the backseat. Hoping to "procure leniency," Billingsley attempted to influence Captain Koch with a unique bribe. Instead of offering money or liquor, the gangster offered the Captain the expensive touring car he was driving at that moment. The state trooper refused to answer. "How would you like a brand new coupe for Mrs. Koch to drive," queried Billingsley next.[180] Captain Koch remained silent. This verbal exchange was shared in the federal circuit court to bolster the government's case against the rumrunning gang. Ultimately, Sherman Billingsley would be convicted on interstate smuggling charges and sentenced to fifteen months in federal prison. His brother Ora would spend two years and a half behind bars. [181]

The Billingsley rumrunning operations, their capture, and the subsequent trial not only revealed the seminal role automobiles played in the earliest days of prohibition in the TDW corridor, but it also demonstrated the importance of developing trans-border relationships. Undoubtedly, the gang needed a fleet of vehicles to transport the alcohol beyond Northwest Ohio, but first the Billingsleys had to "lay the groundwork" with Toledo liquor dealers and Detroit bartenders to ensure they had access to a profitable product and a viable market for their illegal endeavors. The Billingsleys also allowed William Chase to infiltrate their group because they thought he truly was an enterprising middleman whose connections to the Michigan Constabulary would ultimately ensure their economic success without fear of arrest once they crossed state lines.

Just a few days after the successful capture of the Billingsleys, another incident along Monroe County roads indicated that local police—like many other officers around the country—were not properly trained or equipped to enforce dry laws in the age of the automobile. State trooper Harvey Passage was patrolling the so-called Ida Road on his horse just miles north of the state line when two automobiles zoomed up on his position. He stopped the two cars, located sizeable quantities of whiskey, and proceeded to order the rum-running drivers to steer their cars towards Monroe. Passage apparently left behind his horse and entered the second vehicle, barking directions from the back seat. The lead car suddenly "made an effort to escape." The state trooper pulled his gun, shooting it in the direction of the speeding vehicle. After Passage exhausted his ammo, the two bootleggers in the auto he was riding in "jumped on him and beat him into unconsciousness." The pair threw Passage out of the car and left him in a roadside ditch. After regaining consciousness the trooper crawled to a nearby farmhouse where a doctor was summoned. Thirteen stitches later, Passage was taken back to the Michigan State Constabulary headquarters.[182]

As this particular incident evinced, dry agents were often placed in precarious enforcement situations with limited resources, no back up, and little training when confronting motoring criminals early in the Prohibition period. Professional rumrunners frequently traversed in

The paved Dixie Highway as it runs through downtown Monroe. (Photo courtesy the Monroe County Museum)

caravans of autos and a single dry agent, such as Passage, risked his life when attempting to halt and corral liquor law violators transporting booze. His entrance into one of the smuggler's vehicles further demonstrates informal policing and a lack of standard protocols when trying to take control over a motor car involved in an active crime. Moreover, it did not help when individual troopers were without their own automobile or communication methods to call for additional support.

By mid-October, the project to pave the Dixie Highway was finally finished. Being the only completely paved north-south road connecting the Motor City to the Glass City, US-25 became one of the most heavily traveled roads in the country. The *Monroe Evening News* noted that "fall touring" by regional motorists had significantly picked up since the opening of the Dixie. "When the weather is of the right sort there is nothing more healthful than a spin out one of the good roads that radiate from Detroit in all directions," reported the local newspaper. These tourists especially enjoyed the cheap prices on fruit and vegetables that Monroe County farmers offered to the motoring public.[183]

The state troopers charged with enforcing Michigan's dry laws, however, were not enjoying the renovated road system's effects on regional rumrunning. Liquor smuggling by automobile was increasing as violators attempted to blend in with the waves of new traffic. Accordingly, Colonel Vandercook directed an additional squad of state police to guard the roads leading out of Ohio, doubling the total number of dry agents patrolling the Dixie and other north-south roadways to 32. On the first night of ramped up enforcement, one truck and three automobiles were caught collectively hauling close to 100 gallons of booze.[184]

---

[170] "Officers Arrest Auto Smuggler," *Monroe Evening News*, May 8, 1918; "90-Day Sentence Appealed by Pair," *Monroe Evening News*, May 13, 1918; "Whiskey Bottle Flies as Officer Stops Automobile," *Monroe Evening News*, June 20, 1918; "Aims Beer Bottle at Soldier; Fine is Heaviest Yet," *Monroe Evening News*, June 21, 1918.

[171] "State Troops Will Patrol the Toledo Monroe Road Soon," *Monroe Evening News*, June 25, 1918.

[172] "Michigan State Troops Arrived in Monroe Yesterday Afternoon," *Monroe Evening News*, June 28, 1918.

[173] "Every Auto Halted on Patrolled Road by Mounted Police," *Monroe Evening News*, July 1, 1918.

[174] "First Arrests are Made Early Today by Mounted Guard," *Monroe Evening News*, June 29, 1928.

[175] "Every Auto Halted by Mounted Police," *Monroe Evening News*, July 1, 1918; Virginia Scharff, *Taking the Wheel: Women and the Coming of the Motor Age* Albuquerque: University of New Mexico Press, 1991) 135-141.

[176] "Sleeper Commends Sheriff; Says 'We Are Backing You'," *Monroe Evening News*, July 16, 1918.

[177] "Fires Shot at Deputy Sheriff," *Monroe Evening News*, August 12, 1918; "Twenty-Four Are Arrested During Wee Sma' Hours," *Monroe Evening News*, September 14, 1918; "Thirty-Five Were Taken Over Sunday," *Monroe Evening News*, September 16, 1918; "Rumors Regarding Michigan State Troops Thoroughly Sifted," *Monroe Evening News*, September 19, 1918.

[178] Larry Engelmann, "Booze: The Ohio Connection, 1918-1919," *Detroit in Perspective,* vol. II, Winter 1975, 118-119; Phillip Mason, *RumRunning and the Roaring Twenties: Prohibition on the Michigan-Ontario Waterway* (Wayne State University Press: Detroit, 1995), 18.

[179] "Whiskey Bandits Captured Here by State Troops," *Monroe Evening News*, September 30, 1918.

[180] "Booze Agents in Federal Court, One Gives Bail," *Detroit Free Press*, October 1, 1918.

[181] "Red Ink Item: Charge to Whisky 45 Months, $10,000," *Toledo Blade*, January 24, 1919.

[182] "State Trooper Almost Killed by Whiskey Bandits," *Monroe Evening News*, October 2, 1918.

[183] "Tourists Buying from Farmers," *Monroe Evening News,* November 8, 1918.

[184] "Booze Smugglers' Road is Made Much Harder," *Monroe Evening News*, October 8, 1918.

CHAPTER 8
Drying up Detroit: Early Prohibition Enforcement in the Motor City

As officers in Monroe County were bracing themselves for increased activity, a major development in the Buckeye state reaffirmed that the illegal transporting of booze into Michigan would likely only get worse before it got better. On November 5, Ohio voters would go to the polls to decide whether or not the state would follow Michigan's lead and ban booze. There was no doubting how the editorial staff of *The Toledo Blade* felt about the upcoming state prohibition referendum:

> If the end of the earth holds off until the fifth day of November...
> the liquor traffic in Ohio will be voted forever out of business.
> The liquor traffic today has not one reputable friend. It has
> friends to be sure...They are the sort of friends who adorn the
> front and back entrances of barrel houses. They are the friends
> who lie in wait for the bedraggled Michigan stranger, disarrange
> his countenance and pocket his roll, or such part of it as the
> saloon keepers have not already taken.[185]

By a margin of 24,719 votes, Ohio residents decided to dry out the Buckeye State.[186] Toledo's booze industry, consisting of 419 saloons, four breweries, eight wholesale liquor dealers, and nearly 3,000 employees, would be forced to close in May 1919.[187] Despite the fact that notoriously wet Toledo and Lucas County voted against statewide prohibition by

3,972 ballots, the local branch of the Anti-Saloon League collectively convinced the twelve counties and numerous towns in its district to support the referendum by 4,296 margin. Overjoyed, *The Toledo Blade* editorialized, "In no spirit of boastfulness, but with just pride, the Blade

THE END OF A TRAITOR

A cartoon from in the February 1918 edition of *The American Issue* encouraging Ohio voters to ban booze when they go to the polls on November 5, 1918. (Image courtesy University of Michigan, Bentley Historical Library)

recalls the fact that throughout the long years of struggle it has fought unflinchingly for the cause which triumphed Tuesday. It has not been a popular fight, it has cost the Blade much materially. But it was a righteous fight and a just one and the Blade is glad to have served, however feebly or well, in so great a cause."[188]

With just six months remaining of legal alcohol sales in Toledo, area smugglers suddenly felt a renewed sense of urgency to illegally transport booze up to the Motor City. As the election neared, rumrunners flooded the Glass City's "barrel house" district on Monroe Street. Breweries and liquor dealers, who had established close ties to the bootlegging underworld, openly sold booze to known rumrunners from their storefronts, in back alleys, and even from automobiles.[189] A deadly outbreak of the Spanish Influenza during the months of October and November 1918 may have closed up Toledo saloons, but as the *News-Bee* reported, it did not stop automobilized "delivery boys" from supplying their thirsty customers.[190] Immediately after the state prohibition vote, Toledo rumrunners were also caught with increased regularity in November, attempting to profit on legal booze as long as they could.[191]

Perhaps influenced by the influx of motoring smugglers and the on-duty attack of Trooper Passage, area law enforcement officers began to be closely scrutinized for their increasingly aggressive and controversial enforcement tactics. Two state troopers who had previously patrolled roads in Monroe County got themselves in trouble enforcing dry laws in bordering Lenawee County. Attempting to halt a suspected rumrunning vehicle near Hudson, Michigan, the officers "opened fire and punctured a tire and the fenders of the machine."[192] The driver happened to be a former local judge and the passenger was his wife. Infuriated, the ex-judge ordered the Lenawee County sheriff to arrest the two state troopers. The question at hand in the case was whether the Constabulary had the right to use their guns to stop a vehicle and "ascertain whether or not they are transporting liquor." Indeed, troopers had been given explicit orders

from Colonel Vandercook "to stop and search automobiles coming into
Michigan from the direction of Toledo and to shoot holes in the tires

Casey's Wholesale and Retail Liquor store, near Jefferson Avenue and
Superior Street in downtown Toledo, ca 1916. (Photo courtesy the Toledo-
Lucas County Public Library, Images in Time)

of those who fail to stop." Ultimately, the charges were dropped, but the issue of dry agents shooting at motorists unwilling to stop continued throughout the Prohibition years. [193]

Another controversy developed that same fall concerning what happened with rumrunners' automobiles following their arrest. Dry legislation allowed for the temporary confiscation of vehicles utilized in the transportation of booze. During a week and a half period in October, the constabulary "seized nine high-powered automobiles used by bootleggers," near the state line.[194] Nonetheless, a mid-November incident involving a Detroit bootlegger highlighted trooper misbehavior pertaining to these impounded cars. A.J. Muhleisen was arrested with his drinking buddies upon their return from Toledo. Whiskey was found underneath the hood of Muhleisen's Studebaker, the party was escorted to the Monroe jail, and his vehicle confiscated. The Detroiters paid their fines, were released, and the local judge provided the driver a release order to retrieve his car down in Erie, where the Constabulary's garage was located. Once there, however, the vehicle was nowhere to be found. Muhleisen went back to Monroe, spoke with the judge, who in turn made a call to the Constabulary headquarters near Erie. The Studebaker was soon located but upon return "it showed signs of hard usage and the bearings had been burned out." The *Monroe Evening News* interviewed Muhleisen, who clearly voiced his frustrations. "Now the thing that I would like to know is what right have they to use a man's car while he is locked up?" asked the Detroit bootlegger. "I was guilty all right, but have no business using a car that they have no right to. If they are in need of cars to run around in why let the state furnish them."[195]

Muhleisen's rhetorical question actually exposed one of the weaknesses of state prohibition enforcement in its early days. Outfitted with 30 horses, but just one patrol car and a supply truck, the Constabulary lacked the motor power to keep up with the fleets of rum-running vehicles crossing the border every day from northwest

Ohio.[196] Despite the fact that Muhleisen accused them of reckless "joy-riding," state troopers were likely using these confiscated cars for trailing automobilized smugglers. This enforcement tactic was short-lived. On November 26, Michigan's Assistant Attorney General mandated that the Constabulary and other local officers policing the liquor law in southeastern Michigan could no longer utilize seized vehicles for any reason. [197]

Despite the best efforts of the Constabulary near the state line, once rumrunners successfully steered their illegal cargoes through Monroe County many reached their ultimate destination: Detroit. Dry enforcement, especially during the first six months, was lax in and around the Motor City for several reasons. In May, when state prohibition began, Wayne County's prosecutor Charles Jasnowski announced a "tolerant" approach to enforcing the dry laws in the Motor City. The searching of private residences and seizure of alcohol from private citizens would be discouraged. Instead, he ordered his large team of investigators to focus on raiding blind pigs, lower-class bars that continued to illegally serve alcohol. Upper-class establishments—commonly called speakeasies—were rarely targeted in the earliest days of dry enforcement. Considering the metro Detroit area had soundly voted against prohibition, Jasnowski argued that "unreasonable cases, questionable cases, or anything but real prosecutions for straight violations of the state dry law will not survive the scrutiny of a Detroit jury." Noticeably absent from his official statements was anything about pursuing automobiles suspected of transporting alcohol.[198]

Wayne County dry agents, just like their counterparts in Monroe County, were also hindered from doing their job due to a general lack of patrol cars. Chief C.L. Bennett, chief of the county's prohibition inspectors, told the *Detroit Free Press* that his police force was warned about the "needless use of automobiles" by state administrators due to gasoline costs and instead strongly urged to utilize trains and trolleys for tracking down smugglers. Bennett complained, "We can't get down to Trenton to catch early morning bootleggers...without an automobile and we can't work effectively against shipments of liquor unless we can use automobiles to trail the trucks."[199] Bennett was fired a few months later on November 14, 1918. His supervisors jointly stated, "Bennett simply failed to measure up to the requirements of the job" and claimed "liquor was pouring into Wayne County" during his tenure.[200]

His handpicked successor, John Downey, was given much more support and freedom when pursuing automobilized smugglers. Fred L. Woodworth, the State Food and Drug Commissioner who played a large role in handicapping and ousting Bennett, reversed course with Downey at the helm, asserting "I'm going to be a bystander in Detroit. I'm going to let Inspector Downey carry out his own plan in his own way."[201] The ex-superintendent of the Detroit Police Department, Downey had previously directed the "free lance squad" a unique force composed of "a distinctive mobile body" that targeted underworld establishments and figures in the city. On his first day of leading dry enforcement in Detroit, Downey ordered his inspectors to direct their focus on those who were actively running booze into the city. "I don't see what good it does to seize any quantity of smuggled liquor, so long as the men who smuggle it can get away and bring more liquor into the state," declared the chief inspector.[202]

Accordingly, on November 15 the very first arrest under Downey was that of a truck driver who attempted to smuggle 100 gallons of whiskey in ten gasoline cans.[203] In the next couple of days, Downey's inspectors captured rumrunning motorists attempting to bring liquor into Detroit in milk canisters and kegs of oil and another who was transporting by truck 101 barrels of booze hidden among apples from a nearby railyard.[204] The most dramatic bust would occur on the morning of November 18. Downey's men had been hearing of a "green pepper gang" who actively sold liquor at farmers' markets throughout the city. Allegedly, the rumrunning ring was known to sell $5 "extra hot green pepper" bushels that each contained two bottles of whiskey. On the lookout for a particular vegetable truck, dry agents in a patrol car spotted the vehicle heading for Detroit's Eastern Market. Following a "wild pursuit" that spanned over a mile, the officers successfully pulled over the truck, arrested Sam Gianolla and his three accomplices, and confiscated the 41 barrels of liquor hidden among bushel baskets of vegetables. Throughout the remainder of November and December, Downey's dry inspectors were extremely active in their pursuit of autombolized smugglers.[205]

Nevertheless, when it came to drying up the Motor City, ramped up enforcement efforts may have been a case of too little too late. Speakeasies, supposed soft drink saloons, and private individuals had already received significant stocks of alcohol from the organized rumrunning rings that transported illegal supplies from Toledo and beyond. An article published in late November 1918 in the *Toledo Blade* stated while there had been "a slight lowering of the lid" with Downey in control of the prohibition squad, numerous locations throughout Detroit were "still operating as openly as before." The newspaper asserted more than 200 businesses were purveying vast amounts of whiskey and other types of liquor. Beer, on the other hand, was reportedly quite scarce because the profit margins were not as significant and transporting beer in automobiles took up too much cargo space in comparison to more lucrative illegal beverages. Another important feature of "dry" Detroit were the so-called rumrunning plants and depots that dotted the city landscape. Often hidden in plain sight, these locations were frequently visited by automobilized rumrunners who would deliver booze in hidden caches. These plants, in turn, acted as storehouses from which local bootleggers could supply underworld businesses. These "carefully located" plants, that had been in place for months before Downey's tenure, were so well stocked that it would likely take years for Detroit to actually dry out.[206]

As Detroit officials began to take prohibition enforcement more seriously in November and December, officers stationed in Monroe County pressed on with their efforts. Several searches of moving trucks and vans on the Dixie Highway revealed significant caches of alcohol. However, the acquittal of an alleged rumrunner on December 11 demonstrated the unique difficulties of convicting liquor law violators in the automobile age. Toledo resident Frank Pasandy was arrested in mid-November with 30 gallons of booze in his work truck just a couple miles north of the state line. Hired to transport a load of furniture to Wyandotte, Pasandy stated he was unaware that his brother and an acquaintance placed the massive six jugs of alcohol in the back of the vehicle. His twelve-year-old son, a passenger in the truck and called a "clever star witness" by the *Monroe Evening News*, confirmed his father's story "in a straight forward manner." The jury, after deliberating over six hours, came back with a not guilty verdict.[207] As this trial indicated, the numerous hired truck drivers in the region could simply claim ignorance about transporting large amounts of booze for possible vindication. Moreover, a passenger could vouch for the driver's innocence and perhaps expect to be freed of all charges.

Despite the successes of some rumrunners in court and many others who ultimately delivered their illegal supplies to thirsty Detroiters, the Michigan State Constabulary was indeed enforcing the state's dry laws with vigor in the first six months. Throughout the state, troopers arrested 1,102 liquor law violators and 90 percent of these smugglers were captured in Monroe County. Colonel Vandercook also reported that over 17,229 gallons of "red liquor" had been confiscated. The amount of whiskey seized cost rumrunners over $200,000 in the Glass City and would have reportedly fetched $688,000 in the Motor City. Prohibition enforcement officials, especially in Monroe County, were busy in 1918 as indicated by these numbers. Yet with Toledo slated to go dry in just a few months, 1919 would prove to be a momentous year for local dry agents hoping to halt the flood of automobilized smugglers pouring over the Michigan-Ohio state line. [208]

[185] "The End of Booze," *The Toledo Blade*, October 28, 1918.

[186] "Dry Majority in Ohio is 24,719," *The Toledo Blade*, November 14, 1918.

[187] "419 Saloons Knocked Out," *The Toledo Blade,* November 7, 1918.

[188] "A New Day Dawns," *The Toledo Blade*, November 7, 1918.

[189] "Booze Guzzlers Find It Easy to Get Barrel House Liquor," *The Toledo Blade,* October 21, 1918; "Brewer Gave Tip In Raid On 'Leggers," *Toledo News-Bee*, August 1, 1917.

[190] 'Delivery Boys' Jobs Are Easy," *Toledo News-Bee*, October 21, 1918.

[191] "Arrest 2 at Monroe with Load of Liquor," *The Toledo Blade*, November 9, 1918; "Toledoan Bound Over as a Whisky Runner," *The Toledo Blade,* November 9, 1918; "Usual Weekend Haul in Michigan," *The Toledo Blade*, November 25, 1918; "Whiskey Carrier Convicted," *The Toledo Blade,* November 27, 1918.

[192] "Ex-Judge Fights Forcible Search by State Troops," *Monroe Evening News*, November 19, 1918.

[193] "State Troopers Have Been Given Orders to Shoot at Machines Whose Drivers Refuse to Halt," *Monroe Evening News*, November 21, 1918.

[194] "9 Autos, 1682 Quarts of Rum Seized on State Line," *Detroit Free Press*, October 18, 1918.

[195] "Have Troopers Any Right to Use Cars?," *Monroe Evening News*, November 13, 1918.

[196] "State Troopers on Monroe Vigil," *Detroit Free Press*, June 28, 1918; "Rum Guard Camps at Temperance," *Detroit Free Press*, June 29, 1918.

[197] "Pryor, While in Monroe, Says They Have No Right to Use Violator's Cars," *Monroe Evening News*, November 26, 1918.

[198] "Dry Law Sane, Not Ridiculous," *Detroit Free Press*, May 2, 1918.

[199] "Denies Liquor Hunt Impending," *Detroit Free Press*, September 6, 1918.

[200] "Bennett is Out as Rum Nabber," *Detroit Free Press*, November 14, 1918.

[201] "Downey More Powerful, Palmer May Be Retired, As Result of Shakeup," *Detroit Free Press,* December 1, 1914.

[202] "Downey After Rum-Runners," *Detroit Free Press*, November 15, 1918; "Downey 'Foch' In War on Rum," November 16, 1918.

[203] "Odd Circumstances Mark Two Seizures of Whiskey," November 16, 1918.

[204] "Rum Sleuths Make Big Haul of 101 Barrels," *Detroit Free Press*, November 17, 1918.

[205] "Booze Runner Pleads Guilty," *Detroit Free Press*, November 18, 1918; "Raid Nets Rum in 103 Barrels," *Detroit Free Press*, November 20, 1918; "Downey Gets $15,000 in Rum," *Detroit Free Press*, November 21, 1918; "Camouflage Trail Ends in Booze Find," *Detroit Free Press*, December 8, 1918; "Two Careless Persons Held Under Liquor Act," *Detroit Free Press,* December 18, 1918; "Whiskey Worth $50,000 Seized in Record Haul," *Detroit Free Press*, December 23, 1918.

[206] "Is Detroit Dry? Oh, Not So Very," *Toledo Blade,* November 20, 1918.

207 "Youth Caught in the Act by Deputy," *Monroe Evening News*, November 7, 1918; "Moving Van Driver Caught Moving a Big Whiskey Load," *Monroe Evening News*, November 8, 1918; "Nineteen New Ones," *Monroe Evening News*, November 26, 1918; "Truck in Convoy Seized at La Salle," *Monroe Evening News*, December 7, 1918; "Jury Finds Truck Driver Not Guilty," *Monroe Evening News,* December 11, 1918.

208 "State Police Has Made 2,937 Arrests," *Monroe Evening News*, December 23, 1918; "2,937 Arrested by State Police," *Detroit Free Press*, December 22, 1918.

CHAPTER 9
A Winter to Remember

On the night of January 7, 1919, the newly elected Monroe County sheriff, Joseph Bairley, received an anonymous tip that six automobiles loaded with booze had left Toledo for Detroit. Bairley ordered his deputies to guard all of the major bridges on the River Raisin in hopes of catching the caravan. After waiting all night, the officers left their posts at 5:00 a.m. Sure enough, a group of vehicles made their appearance soon thereafter and a "lively chase" ensued for fifteen miles. The suspected rumrunners finally halted after the deputies fired several shots. Close inspection of the cavalcade revealed no liquor in tow and the group was allowed to proceed on to Detroit.[209] It was an inauspicious start to a new year of prohibition enforcement in Monroe County.

Nevertheless, this was not the first prohibition related incident of 1919 in the area. Small-time bootleggers were still using Interurban trolleys and passenger trains to transport themselves and their liquor across state lines. On January 3, dry investigators conducted a massive raid on the local Interurban. Twenty-three liquor violators were taken from the trolley, fourteen of whom were women who were caught with "contrivances" that held bottles under their clothing. Over the course of 1918 and 1919, many smugglers were caught with unique contraptions that hid booze purchased in Toledo. Law enforcers eventually caught on to these deceptive practices. For example, prohibition agents in Monroe County became suspicious of skinny females who left on trolleys or trains and then came back from Toledo just days or even hours later appearing to be several months pregnant. Matron officers were soon hired, and discovered the "expecting" women were actually hiding large flasks of booze around their stomachs. Dolls, hollowed out books, fake loaves of bread, and even false breasts were all found on bootlegging passengers trying to secretly transport alcohol into the Wolverine state.[210]

Despite the incredible ingenuity behind these smuggling devices, the fact that they were being uncovered proved liquor agents were able to effectively police trains and trolleys. Dry detectives had a decided advantage on these transportation systems because they operated on set schedules, schedules that bootleggers had to adhere to as well. Moreover, officers riding with passengers could make calculated deductions about individuals with bulging pockets or garments, clanking suitcases, and nervous dispositions. As bootleggers increasingly were caught, it was reported early on in January that fewer and fewer Interurban tickets were being sold.[211]

In contrast, smugglers held the upper hand over dry agents when hauling a load of liquor in a car. Automobilized rumrunners could decide when to deliver their illegal cargo, whether it was at 5:00 a.m., noon, or a few hours after dusk. Unlike trolleys or trains, with motor vehicles, bootleggers enjoyed the luxury of being able to choose a different route on every run, and even changing their route as they went. The motorized rumrunners could also alter their own speed of travel, driving the speed limit to blend in with normal traffic or speeding up to avoid capture by prohibition officers. The privacy of automobiles, unlike the experience of a passenger riding on a mass transit system, provided rumrunners a convenient barrier between their illegal cargo and nosey dry agents, helping to escape detection. Finally, because of personal ownership of motor vehicles, individual smugglers could tinker with the exterior or interior body of their cars to conceal liquor more discreetly, even when enforcement officials engaged in thorough searches of vehicles. The

A man peers up from the floorboards of a truck that was found smuggling liquor in hidden compartments. (Photo courtesy Wayne State University, Walter P. Reuther Library)

automobile placed rumrunners in the proverbial driver seat of their smuggling endeavors, simultaneously compelling dry officers to become reactionary enforcers rather that proactive policemen. The increasing use of automobiles for TDW corridor rumrunning would significantly challenge Monroe County's liquor law enforcers during the first several months of 1919.

Between January 11 to January 19, 1919 close to 50 automobiles were seized carrying over 3,000 quarts of liquor from Toledo into Monroe County. This was the largest weekly total of rumrunning cars confiscated since the state went dry. Indeed, for the entire month of January, it seemed law enforcement solely focused on automobilized smugglers.[212] Despite these successes, the constabulary and local officers began to commit foolish and serious enforcement errors, primarily due to the usage of motor vehicles in bootlegging.

Shortly before midnight on January 18, a "big booze train" of six vehicles whizzed through downtown Monroe on their way to Detroit. A seventh vehicle in this convoy, however, struck the curb at a busy intersection, disabling the vehicle. The driver fled the scene under a hail of bullets from a Michigan State Constabulary Lieutenant arriving late to the crash scene. The Lieutenant quickly assembled a contingent of troopers and they spent the remainder of the night scouring "the county far and wide" for the missing driver, to no avail.[213] A thorough inspection of the wrecked Paige vehicle revealed a total of 362 quarts of whiskey, several guns, and plenty of ammunition. More interestingly, four sets of license plates from Michigan and Iowa were found in the car. It was soon discovered that the abandoned vehicle had been stolen in Toledo. A wider investigation ensued and it turned out that an eighth vehicle may have played a key role in the "booze train" success. About two miles away from the scene of the downtown accident the driver of the eighth vehicle purposefully stalled his auto near the main Constabulary post guarding the Dixie just before midnight. The troopers naturally converged on the car and while they searched it, the rumrunning "machines speeded by at a rapid rate and got away."[214]

The increasing use of firearms by both prohibition police and automobilized smugglers escalated the enforcement environment in Monroe County as the month of January dragged on. A local deputy sheriff, outfitted with an unmarked patrol car, encountered a couple of Detroit men speeding through downtown Monroe on their motorcycles. In his vehicle, the officer chased the pair south out of town on the Dixie Highway and as they neared the Constabulary post, the troopers stationed there mistook the patrol car for a rumrunning automobile. Shots were fired at the deputy's auto, leaving four bullet holes in the front fender. The motorcyclists were later captured and fined, but the incident underscored how liberal the area's dry agents had become with use of their firearms. In fact, based on *Monroe Evening News* reports in the month of January, local prohibition officers fired their guns on at least six different occasions while enforcing dry laws. Often without their own vehicles, troopers and policemen surmised their best chance of halting bootleggers behind the wheel was to disable their cars by gunfire or at least convey the extreme extent they were willing to engage in to stop illegal smuggling.[215]

Contributing to the increase in firearm usage, armed rumrunners and bandits seemingly multiplied in southern Monroe County. Besides the numerous bootleggers who were caught with weapons in their possession or in their vehicles, "highwaymen" robbed several motorists in Monroe County at gunpoint during the month of January. Caught in the crossfire of dry agents and professional criminals were Monroe County residents and motorists. Newspaper reports indicated that locals who had "no intention of violating the prohibition law are afraid to traverse the 'big paved lane' at nights, fearing that they might be struck by a stray bullet." In fact, earlier in January, a Temperance man was shot in the leg twice while joy riding with his wife on the Dixie Highway near the state line.[216] Farmers in outlying villages and businessmen in downtown Monroe were "terrorized" by the constant shooting and some even began writing lengthy letters of complaint to Governor Sleeper.

Soon thereafter, the state of Michigan and Colonel Vandercook announced that "Little Bertha," an armored vehicle equipped with long-range guns, would help troopers on the Dixie Highway intimidate and halt automobilized liquor violators.[217] On one chilly February night, two *Detroit Free Press* reporters actually covered the late shift with a few of the state troopers. They described the "pot-bellied automobile" as being "built of 3/8-inch steel and weighing 7,000 pounds."[218] The *Toledo News-Bee* also pointed to a unique feature protruding from the front of the vehicle. Little Bertha sported a metal bar fashioned like a "curved knife," stretching from above its covered windshield all the way down to the bumper. Apparently designed for cutting through the barbed-wired frontlines of Belgian battlefields, the armored car's front end would now

Little Bertha, an armored car utilized by the Michigan State Constabulary in their efforts to catch liquor violators along the Michigan-Ohio line. (Photo courtesy the Toledo-Lucas County Public Library, Images in Time)

be used to ram into rumrunning vehicles that refused to stop.[219]

Even with the addition of Little Bertha at the border, February would be a disastrous and humiliating month for prohibition enforcement in Monroe County. Besides the February 7 log incident that resulted in negative publicity and a lawsuit, officers once again got into trouble with their firearms. On February 8, a Milan man brought forward a lawsuit against the Constabulary. The man was driving back from Monroe when a state trooper stopped him and directed a "high-powered rifle" at his head. Despite the fact no booze was found in his vehicle, the officer proceeded to shoot out the car's tires and the gasoline tank. A few days later, prominent Monroe residents clamored for the arrest of two state police officers for firing at their vehicle on the Dixie Highway when they failed to stop. Simultaneously, rumors circulated that a heavily armed band of 300 Detroit autoworkers planned to engage Monroe County's dry agents in a pitched battle just as their new armored vehicle was being mobilized to the state line.[220]

Fred Woodworth, the commissioner of the State Food and Drug Department, revealed in a *Monroe Evening News* interview how bootlegging culture had significantly changed in the early months of 1919. "Amateur" smugglers were now rare and filling the vacuum was a highly organized ring of professional criminals operating on both sides of the Michigan-Ohio line. With established connections to Detroit's underworld, hardened rumrunners found a "nesting place" in Toledo among the "boldest and toughest" criminals in the country who were more than willing to help transport booze and shoot it out with police, according to Woodworth. The commissioner also made note of an "elaborate spy system" in southeastern Michigan that signaled to automobilized bootleggers which roads were guarded, which roads were open, and whether or not to retreat back to Ohio. These professionals could expect to make exorbitant profits if they successfully steered their load to Detroit. Quarts of liquor that cost $3.50 in Toledo could fetch upwards to $13 a bottle in the Motor City.[221]

Beat reporters from the *Toledo Blade* provided insight into the inner workings of the professional criminal culture that was being nourished by profitable trans-border rumrunning. Just a few miles south of the state line, *Blade* journalist Larry Laurence described an interesting scene at "The Last Chance" Saloon. Twenty-five autos lined up in front of the liquor depot ready for their respective load of booze and awaiting orders about which route was "fixed." A few hours later, Laurence received word that all 25 cars successfully made their way to Detroit. The reporter further revealed "day and night automobiles are loaded for interstate transportation" in and around Toledo, increasingly along the lakeshore and the Maumee River. While some motorists employed "little camoflauge" other automobilized smugglers preferred to visit a particular garage in the Glass City before rumrunning jaunts into Michigan. The mechanic there was known to outfit Ford automobiles with liquor concealing pipe coils and copper gasoline tanks partitioned to hide more than five gallons of booze. Anonymous letters sent to local policemen indicated that close to 200 Model T's with rum-filled tanks crossed through Monroe County. Soon thereafter, state troopers began to uncover these specially designed automobiles.[222]

Laurence also made special note of how the "mortgage game" was exploited by regional financiers of smuggling organizations to retrieve motorcars. Dealers of rumrunning vehicles would sell them outright to the bold bootleggers who braved the heavily guarded "Boulevard of Booze," but the dealers would take out mortgages on these cars sold to the rumrunners. In the highly probable event that these cars were wrecked, ditched, or seized by dry agents while transporting illegal cargo, mortgage holders could legitimately reclaim the automobiles they had sold. As mentioned earlier, more and more rum-running cars were being confiscated by state troopers. Nevertheless, a significant number of these automobiles were also being abandoned or involved in accidents.

John Hazele, another *Blade* beat writer, interviewed an Erie, Michigan mechanic who attested to the "scores of cars wrecked along the Dixie Highway" since the state went dry. Evidence indicated the majority of the autos recovered by the mechanic were steered by drunk drivers or rumrunners.[223]

Blade reporters learned that the individuals hauling loads of booze into Michigan were a diverse bunch. Increasingly, local journalists claimed desperate "foreigners" were becoming "the tools" of rumrunning rings. They pointed to the last names of those captured and listed in the jail records in Monroe: "'inskis,' 'owskis,' 'enskis' and a 'harp' filled out the long list." Women were both passengers and drivers in rumrunning vehicles in early 1919. "Women are getting worse...They are carrying whisky in increasing quantities in every conceivable manner," a Michigan dry agent shared. Indeed, one *Blade* reporter literally had a front row seat to these automobilized female booze runners hailing from Toledo. The beat writer was covering the enforcement endeavors of officers in Monroe County when they stopped what appeared to be a family out for a wintertime picnic near the village of LaSalle. The three females, who ranged in age from a teenager to a senior citizen, had chicken sandwiches and jellyrolls, in an effort to give the impression of a wholesome family outing. Upon closer inspection, however, a prodding of the sedan made the cushioned seats "gurgle." Immediately, the constabulary ordered the car confiscated and requested the *Blade* reporter slowly steer the vehicle to the Monroe garage while they followed closely with their shotguns ready. Upon taking the car apart and an "intimate" searching of the females, 30 quarts of rum were found.[224]

The events of January and February demonstrated the significance of automobiles in terms of their impact on rum-running culture. Nevertheless, newspaper reports and existing records do not clearly display how many patrol cars local dry agents possessed in Monroe County in early 1919. In fact, the only mention of vehicles being utilized by troopers or deputy sheriffs occurred when the constabulary acquired their armored vehicle, Little Bertha. One Monroe official, county prosecutor William Haas, made it publicly known that local dry agents not only desired more vehicles, but there was a need for faster vehicles to contend with the influx of automobilized rumrunners. "If the efforts of the state constabulary are to be rewarded and the booze-running problem solved," declared Haas, "the state constabulary must be equipped with high-powered motors at once." The county prosecutor claimed that these new automobiles should have the ability to reach 90 miles per hour to keep pace with their criminal counterparts.[225]

[209] "Sheriff Gets Tip, Bridges Guarded," *Monroe Evening News*, January 7, 1919.

[210] "Inspectors Make Second Big Raid," *Monroe Evening News*, January 3, 1919; Frank Elser, "Keeping Detroit on the Water Wagon," *The Outlook*, vol. 121, 560-561; "Ingenious Devices Employed by Whisky Runners," *Michigan Food and Drug Monthly*, March 1919, 22.

[211] "Inspectors Make Second Big Raid," *Monroe Evening News*, January 3, 1919.

[212] "State Inspectors Bringing Them In," *Monroe Evening News*, January 9, 1919.

[213] "Judge Root Sends Lake Back to Jail," *Monroe Evening News*, January 13, 1919; "Noted Smugglers Caught at Erie," *Monroe Evening News*, January 17, 1919; "State Police Nab Big Amount of Booze," *Monroe Evening News*, January 30, 1919.

[214] "Big Booze Train Evades Troopers," *Monroe Evening News*, January 18, 1919; "Troopers Simply Were Out-Smarted," *Monroe Evening News*, January 21, 1919; "Claimed Abandoned Car Was Stolen," *Monroe Evening News*, January 24, 1919.

[215] "Sheriff Gets Tip, Bridges Guarded," *Monroe Evening News*, January 7, 1919; "Whiskey Runner is Shot in Mouth," *Monroe Evening News*, January 15, 1919; "Big Booze Train Evades Troopers," *Monroe Evening News*, January 18, 1919; "Troopers Simply Were Out-Smarted," *Monroe Evening News*, January 21, 1919; "Police Take Deputy For a Bootlegger," *Monroe Evening News*, January 26, 1919; "Inspectors Handle Detroiter Roughly," *Monroe Evening News*, February 1, 1919.

[216] "Temperance Man Shot in the Leg," *Monroe Evening News*, January 3, 1919.

[217] "The Desperate Efforts Being Made to Kill Troopers Prompts Vandercook to Send 'Little Bertha' Here," *Monroe Evening News*, January 31, 1919.

[218] "Making World Safe For Drys is a Cold Job," *Detroit Free Press*, February 11, 1919.

[219] "It's Better to Stop Than be Stopped by This Auto- Take No Chance," *Toledo News-Bee*, February 24, 1919.

[220] "Troopers' Guns Get Them Into Court," *Monroe Evening News*, February 8, 1919; "Rumor That Auto Workers Would Give Troopers Battle Evidently Prompted Its Being Sent to Border Line," *Monroe Evening News*, February 8, 1919.

[221] "'Professionals' Have Taken the Play Away From 'Amateurs,'" *Monroe Evening News*, February 13, 1919.

[222] "Blade Man Tells of BIg Whisky Run," *Toledo Blade*, February 7, 1919; "Copper Tanks are Specially Made to Carry Booze," *Toledo Blade*, February 12, 1919; "'Quit' Cries Monroe Sheriff; Jail Burst with Rummers," *Toledo Blade*, February 13, 1919.

[223] "Blade Man Tells of Big Whisky Run," *Toledo Blade*, February 7, 1919; "Woman's Rum Car Burned to Hide Evidence," *Toledo Blade*, February 8, 1919.

[224] "Picnic Party Camouflage Fails to Hide Rum in Women's Clothes," *Toledo Blade*, February 6, 1919; "Blade Man Tells of Big Whisky Run," *Toledo Blade*, February 7, 1919; "Plot Against Booze Hounds Hatched Here," *Toledo Blade*, February 10, 1919; "Rum Prisoners Jam Monroe County Jail," *Toledo Blade*, February 10, 1919.

[225] "Police Ask Fast Cars," *Toledo Blade,* Februrary 10, 1919.

CHAPTER 10
The Booze Rush

Shockingly, any automobile would have been useless for dry agents just several days later. On February 18, 1919, a "thunderbolt out of the clear sky" threw open the proverbial rumrunning floodgates. The Michigan State Supreme Court invalidated the Damon Law, the law which prohibited the importation of alcohol into Michigan, largely due to an incident the previous summer on a small island in the Detroit River.[226]

Calf Island was the summer home of multi-millionaire and German newspaper owner August Marxhausen. Inspectors from the Michigan State Food and Drug Department raided his isolated mansion and searched his automobile in August 1918, locating over 6,000 bottles of beer and 38 cases of wine. Marxhausen vehemently opposed the confiscation of his alcoholic supply, claiming that the investigators needed search warrants to legally enter his home and vehicle and, in turn, seize his booze.[227] After months of lower court decisions and appeals, the case made its way to Michigan's Supreme Court. The Court declared, "that while the manufacture, sale or purchase of liquor is still prohibited, possession of liquor is not contrary to law and a man in possession of liquor cannot be molested by unwarranted search or seizure."[228]

Consequently, the so-called "Booze Rush" ensued. Professional and amateur rumrunners alike invaded the "fountains of delight" in the Glass City, prompting the Toledo police to remark "they had never saw such a stream of autos." As it could be predicted, downtown liquor stores benefited the most from the "lifting of the lid," as smugglers looked to profit from their now legal endeavors. Business was so brisk for some wholesale dealers that they discontinued supplying local bars for a few days, figuring they could make significant sums of money without this major component of regular operations. Salesmen could not stock the liquor display shelves fast enough and they even refused to engage in haggling with cheap bootleggers. The demand for booze was so high that the sale price for a quart jumped from $1 to $3 and the high quality stuff went for $6. The price for a case of whiskey increased by $7, and at $30 a case it was estimated that liquor dealers had sold 200,000 cases in just three days. Toledo bank administrators reported that the deposits of cash, primarily from saloonkeepers and wholesale liquor house operators, were the "largest in the history of Toledo."[229]

The "abnormal conditions" benefited many other businesses in the Glass City, especially restaurants and hotels. Thousands of local residents came out to witness the commotion and "watch the free shows that were being staged at all depots, on the streets, and around liquor stores and saloons." These gawkers subsequently made a night of it, visiting the city's many fine dining spots. The numerous rumrunners who were not able to secure their alcoholic supply or a mode of transportation north filled Toledo's hotels. Those who could not obtain a room attempted to find a place to rest within downtown lunchrooms or slept out on the streets on top of their suitcases.[230]

Demonstrating the importance of automobiles during the two-day "Booze Rush," Glass City mechanic garages and taxicab lines were also swamped with customers. Nearby Sandusky, Ohio automobile dealers reported that they had sold out of their entire stock of fast cars to men admitting to represent professional whiskey smugglers. Many small-time bootleggers opted to transport their booze by Interurban or passenger train, but those who desired to make significant profits knew that smuggling by motorcar was their best option. On February 18, Toledo area motorists, due to their proximity to a wet source, were the first to load up their cars and head north on roadways into Michigan. Next, during the early hours of February 19, a flood of Michigan vehicles descended upon the Glass City. Midnight spectators in downtown Monroe counted 75 cars zooming through their town in one hour, an incredible rate for that location during that time period. The demand was so high that trucks from Cleveland were called into Toledo to replenish the city's depleted supply of booze. The *Detroit Free Press* subsequently claimed that "autos by the hundred" were pouring into Michigan from Toledo. Heavy trucks, fancy touring cars, and even horse drawn carriages left Northwest Ohio fully loaded with liquor.[231]

Just north of the state line, booze running, bumper-to-bumper traffic and numerous automobile accidents captured significant media attention. The Dixie Highway was the scene of much of the roadside drama. Impatient motorists on the two-lane road resulted in a reported 53 wrecks. Enterprising mechanics mobilized themselves and made handsome profits assisting disabled whiskey runners. The *Toledo News-Bee* published photos of the congested traffic, the autos that were abandoned in the ditch, and even created a cartoon lampooning the recklessness of the automobilized rumrunners.[232]

Not everyone found the Booze Rush humorous. As one Monroe County farmer noted, the noisy nighttime motorcar traffic resulted in bouts of sleeplessness. One Monroe taxi driver seriously injured his smuggling passengers when his car careened off the road. Twenty-eight Toledo residents had their cars stolen and utilized for rumrunning purposes. A *Detroit Free Press* photographer went down to southern Monroe County to take pictures of the vehicles strewn about the side of the Dixie only to find a very familiar auto. A bootlegger had stolen the photographer's touring car, and while used it to smuggle booze back to Detroit, ended up steering the automobile into a ditch south of Erie, Michigan.[233]

For 48 hours, dry agents stationed in Monroe could only watch on as liquor-toting shenanigans happened all around them. Anticipating the massive profits they were about to earn, vehicular rumrunners loudly sang impromptu tunes out their windows such as "We Are No Longer Dry" and "Hello Monroe, Hello Detroit."[234] Other motoring smugglers rolled through downtown mockingly asking for directions

The front page of the February 21, 1919 edition of the *Toledo News-Bee* documents the chaos of the Booze Rush the preceding day. (Image courtesy the Toledo-Lucas County Public Library, Images in Time)

whenever they encountered an officer patrolling the sidewalks. A few bold truck drivers with hundreds of quarts in tow stopped in full view of law enforcement and opted to engage in some downtown shopping. Donald Childs, captain of the constabulary's Monroe contingent, frustratingly claimed all he could do "was sit on his hands and wait" and Childs ordered his troopers to do the same. [235]

At first, Monroe residents were entertained by the bizarre spectacle

A cartoon from the February 22, 1919 edition of the *Toledo News-Bee* poking fun at the Booze Rush earlier in the week. (Image courtesy the Toledo-Lucas County Public Library, Images in Time)

occurring in their hometown, packing the busy sidewalks to capture glimpses of the continuous flow of rumrunners. However, as the Booze Rush continued on for a second day and a record 390 whiskey-laden cars an hour filtered through Monroe, local citizens became annoyed by all of the commotion consuming their quaint city. A *Monroe Evening News* reporter declared that the "constant stream" made "Woodward Avenue in Detroit look like a deserted lane."[236] Just a week earlier, many in Southeast Michigan were complaining about the overzealous efforts of dry agents. Now, they begged for law enforcement to do anything they could to halt the liquor traffic. Yet, with the Michigan Supreme Court invalidating the search of automobiles and seizure of alcoholic cargo, little could be done by local officers. In comparison to the previous nine months of stringent dry policing, the "Booze Rush" had seemingly turned the county's enforcement culture upside-down.[237]

Meanwhile in Detroit and the surrounding suburbs, truckloads of alcohol were being openly delivered to private citizens and proprietors of local speakeasies. Restaurants and jazz clubs overflowed with patrons and intoxicating beverages. The *Detroit Free Press* reported there was now more alcohol in supposedly dry Detroit and its neighboring communities than in wet Toledo. Nonetheless, during the two-day spree, reckless motorists around Detroit wreaked havoc on the streets. On February 20, three men driving a liquor-laden vehicle through Wyandotte crashed into an Interurban. The motorcar was dragged two blocks and the trolley mangled the lifeless bodies of two of the rumrunners. The third man would die a half hour later from a crushed skull.[238]

Later that day, in a Detroit area safety zone, designed to reduce reckless driving and prevent pedestrian fatalities, a drunken bootlegger struck and killed an 11-year-old girl with his vehicle. A local journal placed blame not only on the individual behind the wheel but the culture of automobilized smuggling that had pervaded the region. "The fine abandon and cheerful, 'good-time' uproariously of liquor-running is forever stained with blood," declared the *Michigan Food and Drug Monthly*. "Barleycorn's juggernaut, as it careened riotously along last February, collected pitiful dark masks on its whirling wheels." The journal finished its editorial by urging the state's citizens to fully embrace the existing dry laws, stating, "A common effort to support the state in this mandate will suppress the liquor-running that murders innocents and keep Michigan proof against ridicule." [239]

Embarrassed by the entire debacle, Governor Sleeper, Colonel Vandercook, and other dry legislators and leaders in Michigan convened in Lansing and Monroe for emergency meetings on February 18, 19, and 20. Together they cobbled up a plan for "plugging up the leak" that had been flooding the Toledo-Detroit corridor. The state's existing Wiley Act, which effectively outlined how state prohibition in Michigan would be enforced, was quickly modified on February 20. This enabled Monroe County's Circuit Court judge, Jesse Root, to deputize troopers and members of the sheriff's office to arrest those coming into Michigan with illegal alcohol. More drastically, they decided the Reed Act, a federal law that criminalized interstate transportation of alcohol into dry territory, should also be utilized. Accordingly, U.S. marshals and Michigan Constabulary troopers were allowed to "set up shop" along the state line and nab as many violators as possible. Thirty automobilized rumrunners were captured and 24 vehicles seize on the first full day. Along with these arrests, they would collectively confiscate "Four barrels, 309 cases, twenty gunny sacks, 23 suitcases, eight jugs, and 150 bottles of whiskey." [240]

Nonetheless, not all motorists stopped were rumrunners. On February 22, seven more vehicles were found to be carrying booze into Michigan, but one "small but high-powered car" approached the position of the dry agents at a creep. Then, all of the sudden, the driver pressed on the gas and "rushed for the open highway." The officers shot at the fleeing automobile, alerting "the battered police truck" to block the road. The motorcar came to a stop and a thorough search revealed that there was no liquor in tow. The male driver apparently was fearful of armed robbers and automobile thieves lurking along the highway and decided to make his get-away. The man was arrested for "resisting an officer."[241]

Detroit city policemen also began to take matters into their own hands by actively patrolling the corner of Griswold and Fort, where many bootleggers stepped off the Interurban with suitcases, boxes, and other devices. Starting on February 20, officers slyly began asking smugglers what they were carrying and if they admitted to be transporting booze, the bootlegger was arrested and the liquor confiscated. Thousands of quarts of booze piled up behind the police and crowds of Detroiters watched on with amusement. Word soon filtered throughout the city that law enforcement was once again enforcing dry laws. Cab drivers quickly swarmed around the policing site and bootleggers "in the know" flagged them down, handed them a wad of cash, and took off with their alcoholic supply secure. Apparently, the lack of automobiles on hand for these officers made their efforts less effective. The *Detroit Free Press* reported that the liquor law enforcers only had a few "patrol wagons and private machines" to transport the confiscated booze from the street corner curb to the downtown police station. Bottles and packages sat for hours on the sidewalk, enabling enterprising thieves to snatch several quarts at a time and take off in waiting taxis.

Despite these setbacks, Detroit area dry agents expanded their endeavors over the course of the next few days throughout the city and into the suburbs, raiding blind pigs, restaurants openly serving alcohol, and other locales holding liquor and beer caches. With local, state, and federal agents all working to enforce liquor laws throughout the region, the "Booze Rush" was effectively reduced to a trickle by the end of February.[242]

226 "State Calls in Liquor Guards Under Supreme Court Rule," *Detroit Free Press*, February 19, 1919.

227 "6,000 Bottles of Beer Seized on Calf Island," *Detroit Free Press*, August 3, 1919.

228 "Abend Post Owner Pleads Not Guilty," *Detroit Free Press*, October 11, 1918; "New Marxhausen Case Adjourned Until Jan. 20," *Detroit Free Press*, December 21, 1918.

229 "Court Outlaws Booze Search," *Toledo News-Bee*, February 19, 1919; "Floating Down the Old Green River," *Toledo News-Bee*, February 20, 1919; "Toledo Near Dry; Detroit Very Wet," *Detroit Free Press*, February 19, 1919; "Receipt From Whisky Sales Last Few Days Estimated at $6,000,000," *Toledo News Bee*, February 21, 1919; "Detroiters Furnish a Lot of Laughs for Toledo Folks," *Toledo News Bee*, February 21, 1919.

230 "Detroiters Furnish a Lot of Laughs for Toledo Folks," *Toledo News Bee*, February 21, 1919.

231 "Court Outlaws Booze Search," *Toledo News Bee*, February 19, 1919; "Michigan-Ohio Line Guarded for Liquor Smugglers," *Austin American-Statesman*, February 21, 1919; "Booze Running Short in Toledo Because of Demand for Michigan," *Sandusky Star-Journal*, February 21, 1919; "Toledo Warehouses Pour Red Stream Into Michigan," *Detroit Free Press*, February 19, 1919.

232 "The Booze Caravan and Some Dashed Hopes," *Toledo News Bee*, February 21, 1919; "Michigan or Bust," *Toledo News Bee*, February 22, 1919.

233 "Court Outlaws Booze Search," *Toledo News Bee*, February 19, 1919; "Toledo's Stock of Rum Fading," *Detroit Free Press*, February 22, 1919.

234 "Liquor Violators Walk Out of Monroe County Jail, Monroe is Rapidly Being Flooded with Booze" *Monroe Evening News*, February 19, 1919.

235 "Liquor Flows Unresisted in Detroit," *Detroit Free Press*, February 20, 1919.

236 "Federal Sleuths Now Stationed at the Ohio Border," *Monroe Evening News,* February 20, 1919.

237 "Liquor Flows Unresisted in Detroit," *Detroit Free Press*, February 20, 1919.

238 "Auto Numbers Taken at Line," *Detroit Free Press*, February 21, 1919.

239 "Toledo Near Dry; Detroit Very Wet," *Detroit Free Press*, February 20, 1919; "Detroit Police Seize Whiskey," *Detroit Free Press*, February 21, 1919; "Three Killed in Booze Rush in Michigan," *Binghamton Press*, February 21, 1919; "Auto Driver Declares Innonence in Killing," *Detroit Free Press*, February 21, 1919; "Editorial," *Michigan Food and Drug Monthly*, April 1919, 6.

240 "Dry Forces Meet While Booze Flows," *Monroe Evening News*, February 21, 1919; "Federal Officers Mix in Michigan Fight," *The American Issue*, March 1, 1919.

241 "Car and Cafe Raids by Detroit's Police Halt Liquor's Flow," *Detroit Free Press*, February 23, 1919.

242 "Detroit Police Seize Whiskey," *Detroit Free Press*, February 21, 1919; "Car and Cafe Raids by Detroit's Police Halt Liquor's Flow," *Detroit Free Press*, February 23, 1919; "Runners Afraid of Uncle Samuel," *Monroe Evening News*, February 25, 1919.

CHAPTER 11
"Plugging Up the Leak:" Toledo Goes Dry

Despite an increased enforcement presence along the Michigan-Ohio border, professional rumrunners were still being chased after and arrested throughout the spring of 1919. With Toledo and the rest of Ohio slated to go dry in May, local residents surmised their time to profit from the illegal liquor trade was limited. Newspaper reports suggest that fewer bootleggers opted to utilize regional mass transit systems during the three-month span between the Booze Rush and Ohio's dry date, perhaps due to the inherent inability to transport larger caches of alcohol on trolleys and trains. Simultaneously, the numerous motorcar smugglers arrested during this time period attest to the massive loads of liquor rumrunners were attempting to bring into the Wolverine state.[243] On the outskirts of Monroe, two men and two women in a vehicle were arrested on March 4 with 400 quarts of whiskey and ten cases of beer.[244] A week later a Detroit motorist was caught in his motorcar on the Dixie Highway trying to deliver 308 quarts of "firewater" to the Motor City.[245] The *Monroe Evening News* consistently wrote of vehicles that were filled "to the guards" or "heavily loaded" with gallons of intoxicating beverages. Much to dry agents' chagrin, newspaper reports also shared that numerous rumrunners in the area were able to escape prohibition officers' efforts to detain them. While some were able to zoom past guarded checkpoints, a handful of others traveling with convoys daringly abandoned loaded automobiles and jumped into another smuggling motorcar.[246]

With rumors circulating that "higher ups" and "reputed millionaires" were teaming up with criminal smuggling operations, dry legislators in Michigan proposed and passed a stringent prohibition law in the spring of 1919, one that took direct aim at rumrunners' automobiles.[247] The law allowed state circuit courts "to issue blanket injunctions" against smugglers transporting alcohol into Michigan, resulting in automatic confiscation of vehicles involved.[248]

A few weeks later, another piece of legislation was brought to the floor, calling for the official transfer of bootleggers' "booze cars" to the state government. Both Commander Vandercook of the Michigan Constabulary and Commissioner Woodworth of the State Food and Drug Department advocated on behalf of the proposed legislation. Vandercook said he believed automobiles were key to rumrunning culture, stating that "once the cars are taken away from the smugglers the illicit traffic will be reduced to a minimum." A few days later, Governor Sleeper signed the Lewis Bill—named after ardent dry advocate and Michigan Representative Lynn Lewis—which included provisions that enabled the confiscation and permanent seizure of automobiles used in transporting liquor.[249]

The rumrunners themselves also faced harsher penalties under what was called the "most drastic dry law ever passed." The Lewis Bill elevated every prohibition violation from a misdemeanor to a felony. Each violator charged would be subject to a $1,000 fine and a prison term of at least six months. Additionally, because liquor violations were now a felony, dry agents' use of firearms was legally protected when confronting vehicles full of booze.[250]

While the stakes were raised for liquor smugglers, accusations of bribery and corruption troubled those enforcing local prohibition laws.

State troopers stationed in southern Monroe County admitted in March 1919 that "hardly a day passes" without being offered a handsome bribe from a rumrunner.[251] A few months later, Sergeant Arthur Muttin of the Michigan Constabulary was charged with extorting a bribe near the state line from female bootleggers who possessed a gallon and a half of whiskey in their car.[252] Some law enforcement officials in the region were caught partaking in the smuggling and selling of illegal alcohol themselves. Monroe County's sheriff, Joseph Bairley, was ultimately relieved of his post by Governor Sleeper after eye witnesses testified Bairley was found driving drunk near the state line and selling confiscated liquor from his residence. One of the primary investigators working the Billingsley case the previous fall was sentenced to eighteen months in federal prison for operating a professional liquor smuggling ring that operated between Milwaukee and Grand Rapids, Michigan. And even though they were never charged, state troopers suspected Detroit policemen—who were often unwilling to allow a search of their motorcars when returning from Toledo—of engaging in the illegal alcohol trade.[253]

A few weeks later, a shocking incident on the Dixie Highway in the small town of Erie, Michigan, just a few miles over the state line, seemingly validated the need for stringent dry laws and steadfast enforcement.

Early in the morning of April 29, 1919 a local teenage girl was waiting on the edge of the Dixie Highway for the 7:24 a.m. interurban. At that moment, a hay wagon pulled out in front of a rumrunner that was roaring up the highway in a Studebaker. Attempting to avoid a collision with the farmer, the rumrunner instead slammed into the girl, killing her instantly.[254] The bootleggers sped away, but they knew witnesses in the town had ample time to read their license plate. Subsequently, once they traveled a distance up the road, the pair of rumrunners ditched their car, tore off the license plate, and took off on foot. Captured a few hours later by police, it turned out that the driver was Louis Harris, a Toledo bartender, and his passenger was Ernest Perkis, a Detroit "whiskey-runner." When recovering the "abandoned machine," officers found 36 pints of whiskey ingeniously concealed in the frame of the car. Harris was ultimately charged with manslaughter and sentenced to ten years in prison.[255]

The deadly accident in Erie foreshadowed the desperate, last-ditch attempts by criminal bootleggers to procure available supplies of alcohol before Ohio's "bone dry" date of May 27, 1919. Just a couple of weeks later, on May 14, the United States government called for an auction in Toledo to sell the "estate" of booze confiscated in Michigan, which included thousands of quarts of whiskey and gin. Ironically, some bootleggers who had previously lost their liquor supply to law enforcement across the border could now buy it back just before Ohio went dry. According to the *Toledo News-Bee*, interest in the auction was "indicated by the hundreds of calls" received by the local IRS office.[256]

Outright theft was another method of liquor acquisition practiced by professional rumrunners in the weeks leading up to the state's new prohibition law. To begin the month of May, one particular incident illuminated the extent to which the bootlegging culture had spread in Toledo. On the morning of May 1, three members of the Toledo Police Department attempted to steal $5,000 worth of whiskey from the "storeroom" of a downtown hotel. At first, the three officers and their taxi chauffeur had seemingly pulled off the heist and "made way with several auto loads of whiskey." Soon thereafter, however, more than a dozen of the cases were stolen from the taxi driver accomplice, causing him to openly accuse other chauffeurs of taking his new supply. Overheard on the streets by TPD detectives, the taxi man was subsequently brought in for questioning. The plot quickly unraveled and soon the three officers were implicated in a whiskey smuggling ring. Several newspaper reports indicate that the stealing of large caches of alcohol continued as the state prohibition date approached.[257]

On Toledo's final day of drinking, the dry community began to fully celebrate what seemed to be the impending deathblow to "John Barleycorn."[258] Several downtown churches held special services for the event. Many dry dignitaries, including the superintendent of the Ohio Anti-Saloon League, were in the Glass City. St. Paul's Methodist Church commemorated "Barleycorn's" "funeral" by inviting a nationally-renown lecturer to speak to their congregation. Marry Harris Armour, fittingly known as the "Georgia Cyclone," shouting and rambling "at a mile a minute" pace, shared her extreme prohibitionist views with those in attendance. Besides claiming alcohol was the root cause of insanity

A photo on the front page of the May 24, 1919 edition of the *Toledo News-Bee* documents "some of Old Man Booze's mourners taking 'one last, fond look' at the 'remains' in the windows of a downtown liquor house." (Image courtesy the Toledo-Lucas County Public Library, Images in Time)

and saloonkeepers were not welcome in heaven, Armour justified the congregation's early jubilation. "We are not rejoicing prematurely," Armour affirmed. "It takes a thousand times as much time to undo things as to do them. It has taken us 79 years to do what we have done and it will take the wets 79,000 years to undo it."[259]

Prohibitionists in Toledo were not the only ones pleased with the drying out of the Glass City. For the first time in over a year, police officers and government officials in Monroe County reportedly were able to "sit around and swap yarns" with each other without the prospect of having to deal with a rumrunner on the roadway or in the courthouse.[260] Detroit police officers were relieved as well, considering the previous month's 541 motorcar "smash-ups" within the city's limits were primarily caused by intoxicated Detroiters returning from Toledo. They were especially "hopeful" that Ohio's prohibition law would significantly reduce the number of accidents concentrated where motorists entered Detroit from the infamous Dixie Highway. While some expected a renewal of smuggling activities in the future, other dry agents in the region predicted "that the old days are gone forever."[261]

Indeed, the steady stream of automobilized bootleggers flowing over the state line was now reduced to a trickle, effecting the jobs of those charged with enforcing the state's prohibition laws. Only a handful of motorists were caught rumrunning in the summer of 1919 in Monroe County and officers stationed in the area increasingly resorted to raiding houses, shacks, and junkyards for illegal supplies of booze.[262] With little work to do, dry inspectors from the Michigan State Food and Drug Department at first declared they would be taking a "back seat" to federal prohibition agents who had stayed on since the Booze Rush days three months earlier. Fred Woodworth, the department's commissioner said, "I am firmly of the view that a dry law can be most efficiently enforced by federal officials, as nine-tenths of the cases extend over state lines." A couple days later, a dispatch from Lansing indicated that the state's inspectors were pulled from Monroe County altogether due to the fact "that the shipments of liquor from Ohio have practically ceased."[263]

The Michigan Constabulary was also ultimately relieved of their enforcement duties throughout the county. The townspeople of Dundee, Michigan—who overwhelmingly voted in favor of the state prohibition measure—became disgruntled when troopers began to arrest farmers for minor traffic violations in the downtown district.[264] Rural motorists brought their business elsewhere and the proprietors of downtown Dundee clamored for the removal of the state police stationed in and around their town. On July 17, Monroe County prosecutor William Haas argued on behalf of Dundee's residents, penning a letter to Colonel Vandercook of the Constabulary. "The men of this troop have made no arrests for a great many months for violation of the liquor law," Haas pointed out. He continued, "Surely a little village like Dundee which has had only such police protection as one old night watchman…does not at this time need a whole troop of state police to look after it."[265] Vandercook agreed and the troopers were removed from Dundee the next day. About a month later, Vandercook decided to relocate the remainder of his troopers stationed just north of the state line. The *Monroe Evening News* noted it "was no longer necessary" for the state police to guard the border because "whiskey is become [sic] more scarce in Toledo with each succeeding day."[266]

Dry agents in Monroe County likely left their posts with a sense of accomplishment. The rampant rumrunning in the region had been quelled to the point they were no longer needed, at least for the time being. The officers were also were responsible for the vast majority of the 2,338 men and women who were arrested and brought up on charges in the county's circuit court during the first six months of 1919, a record to that point.[267] The yearlong efforts of the dry agents and their bootlegging counterparts in the region—especially the two-day rumrunning spree in February—had other significant and far-reaching effects. Amusing and desperate tales of liquor smugglers in Lucas, Monroe, and Wayne Counties filled newspapers throughout the nation. Photos of state troopers searching cars and operating Little Bertha filtered out to towns around the Midwest. Images of the "Booze Rush" even made its way onto the big screen in Detroit's downtown theaters. Michigan's dry experiment was closely watched around the country and reports of the rampant rum running revealed that large urbanized areas would not go down without a fight and numerous intoxicating beverages. Henry Ford, in his company-owned *Dearborn Independent*, clamored for fewer/ lower fines and more jail time for liquor law violators. The Anti-Saloon League expressed concern in its nationally syndicated periodical that the situation in Monroe County might give "new impetus to the whiskey running profession."[268]

Perhaps more importantly, for those directly involved in the smuggling, the officers enforcing local prohibition laws, or the TDW residents who watched firsthand, the major lessons learned pertained to the resources and methods on display. Locals could easily deduce that the ongoing war over the illegal transportation of alcohol would be won by those who utilized automobiles more effectively. Considering that regional dry agents barely had access to cars—let alone high-quality ones—it was clear bootleggers on the TDW corridor possessed a decided advantage.

---

[243] "Big Bootleggers Resume Operation," *Monroe Evening News*, March 4, 1919.

[244] "State Police Make a Big Haul Today," *Monroe Evening News*, March 4, 1919.

[245] "Army Officer is Arrested by Police," *Monroe Evening News*, March 12, 1919

[246] "Three Cars Get By, Five Are Seized," *Monroe Evening News*, March 13, 1919; "Many Cars, Containing Much Liquor Seized Over Sabbath. Bribe Money Again Making Appearance," *Monroe Evening News*, March 17, 1919; "Temperance People All Agog Over Arrival of Reputed Millionaires. Three Cars Get Away," *Monroe Evening News*, March 20, 1919.

[247] "Temperance People All Agog Over Arrival of Reputed Millionaires. Three Cars Get Away," *Monroe Evening News*, March 20, 1919; "Toledo 'Higher-Ups' Picked Up By Police," *Monroe Evening News*, March 24, 1919

[248] "Bill Would Permit Seizure of Cars," *Monroe Evening News*, March 9, 1919.

[249] "New Bill Aimed at the Booze Cars," *Monroe Evening News*, March 27, 1919; "Most Drastic Law Ever Passed," *Monroe Evening News*, April 2, 1919.

[250] "Assistant Attorney General Baillie Contends That the Troopers Have Right to Shoot Under Lewis Law," *Monroe Evening News,* April 3, 1919.

[251] "Many Cars, Containing Much Liquor Seized Over Sabbath; Bribe Money Again Making Appearance," *Monroe Evening News*, March 17, 1919.

[252] "Trooper Charged with Taking Bribe," *Monroe Evening News*, May 24, 1919; "Sheriff Sold Liquor, Claim," *Detroit Free Press*, April 12, 1919.

[253] "Governor Sleeper Orders Bairley to Step Down and Out," *Monroe Evening News*, July 10, 1919; "Says Love of Gain Led Him Astray," *Monroe Evening News*, April 25, 1919.

[254] "Girl Killed by Whisky-Laden Car", *Toledo Blade*, April 29, 1919; "Girl Killed by Speeding Auto; Two Men Held", *Toledo News-Bee*, April 29, 1919.

[255] "'Too Nervous to Stop,' Says Driver," *Monroe Evening News*, April 29, 1919; "Whiskey Car Kills Girl Near Monroe," *Detroit Free Press*, April 30, 1919; "Charge of Murder Preferred Against Louis Harris Reduced to Manslaughter," *Monroe Evening News*, December 10, 1919.

[256] "Dry Majority in Ohio is 24,719" *Toledo Blade*, November 14, 1918; "John Barleycorn on Auction Block", *Toledo News-Bee*, May 13, 1919.

[257] "Patrol-Men Held in $5,000 Whisky Theft", *Toledo News-Bee,* May 2, 1919; "Thieves Get Whisky and Jewelry" *Toledo News-Bee*, May 16, 1919; "Forced to Leave Booze; Robbed", *Toledo News-Bee*, May 23, 1919; "Steal $400 Worth of Wine from Café", *Toledo News-Bee*, 1919.

[258] "Caberet Girls to Chant J. Barleycorn's Requiem as Mourner's Weep—and Drink", *Toledo News-Bee*, May 24, 1919.

[259] "Post-Mortem is Due on Booze", *Toledo News-Bee*, May 24, 1919; "Exult at Death of Booze", *Toledo News-Bee*, May 26, 1919.

[260] "County Officials Kept Constantly on Jump by Rum Runners Now Able to Sit Around and Swap Yarns," *Monroe Evening News*, May 29, 1919.

[261] "Hope to Check Fatal Wrecks," *Detroit Free Press*, May 26, 1919.

[262] "Four Runners Are Nabbed, 1 Gets Away," *Monroe Evening News*, July 7, 1919; "Inspectors Raid Three Junk Yards," *Monroe Evening News*, June 23, 1919; "Inspectors Raid Fishermen Homes," *Monroe Evening News*, August 1, 1919.

[263] "Woodworth's Men to Take Back Seat," *Monroe Evening News*, July 3, 1919; "Sleuths Dropped No Longer Needed," *Monroe Evening News*, July 5, 1919; "Rum Runners Are So Few That State Troopers Leave," *Monroe Evening News,* August 22, 1919.

[264] "Dundee Seeking Troopers Removal," *Monroe Evening News*, July 15, 1919.

[265] "Night Watchman Enough Says Haas," *Monroe Evening News,* July 17, 1919.

[266] "Troopers Removed from Dundee," *Monroe Evening News*, July 18, 1919; "Woodworth's Men to Take Back Seat," *Monroe Evening News*, July 3, 1919; "Sleuths Dropped No Longer Needed," *Monroe Evening News*, July 5, 1919; "Rum Runners Are So Few That State Troopers Leave," *Monroe Evening News,* August 22, 1919.

[267] "Over 2,300 Arrests Made in 6 Months," *Monroe Evening News*, July 8, 1919.

[268] "Court Hits Dry Law and Flow of Liquor Makes Detroit Glad," *Pittsburgh Gazette*, February 20, 1919; "Whisky Trail to Detroit is Deadly to Three; Autos Race with Booze," *Oregon Journal*, February 20, 1919; "Rum Flows in Mighty Stream to Michigan," *Salt Lake Herald*, February 21, 1919; "Raid Runners in Michigan," *New York Times*, February 21, 1919; "What the Supreme Court Stopped," *Sheboygan Press*, February 21, 1919; "Stop War on Bootleggers," *Evansville Press*, February 25, 1919; "'Got Whisky?'- 'Nope' - 'Drive On'", *Muncie Evening Press*, February 22, 1919; "Scenes Along Wet Highway Shown in Free Press Film," *Detroit Free Press*, February 23, 1919; "Add Thirty Days," *Dearborn Independent*, February 13, 1919; "Federal Officers Mix in Michigan Fight," *The American Issue*, March 1, 1919.

CHAPTER 12
Changing Lanes: Canadian Booze Traffic and the Beginning of National Prohibition

On the morning of May 13, 1920, a pair of sheriff deputies, Flicker and Metz, were patrolling the Dixie Highway in northern Monroe County near Newport, a small farming village on the shores of Lake Erie. Metz's automobile broke down and Flicker, an ex-machinist, was attempting to make the necessary repairs when a "large Cadillac car bearing an Illinois license" zoomed by their position. Metz instantaneously remarked "there goes a booze car." Flicker decided to give chase on his motorcycle, stopping the suspected rumrunner's vehicle in front of Newport's most prominent general store and a gawking crowd of approximately twenty locals. The deputy sheriff walked up to the car and declared that the driver would be arrested for speeding. Suddenly three armed gunmen surrounded Flicker, overwhelmed him, and shoved him into their Cadillac.

Once inside the vehicle, Deputy Flicker made note of the fact that there was no sign of any liquor and that these gunmen from Chicago—ranging in age from 25 to 35—were apparently on some kind of "job" or business trip. After meandering through Monroe County's backroads for an hour and a half, the gangsters forced Flicker to point out the way to Detroit, deliberately avoiding any village and for good reason. After telephone operators quickly sent out a notification, police armed with sawed off shotguns actively searched for the Cadillac throughout the Toledo, Monroe County, and Detroit areas. Flicker was repeatedly asked about the conditions of the highways they would travel on, demonstrating perhaps the gunmen's concerns about their vehicle experiencing difficulty due to rough roads. Once they reached the western limits of Detroit, Flicker's gun was unloaded, handed back to him, and he was thrown out of the car.[269]

Flicker caught an Interurban back to Monroe and arrived in his hometown around 7:00 p.m. It was undoubtedly the most interesting eight hours of his professional career. Newspaper reporters from Monroe and Toledo gathered around him, bombarding him with questions but Flicker refused to speak at length about the ordeal. Nevertheless, the *Toledo News-Bee* reported it was the collective belief of southeast Michigan and northwest Ohio police that the gunmen were "connected to the killing of Jim Colosimo, king of Chicago's underworld." Indeed,

Downtown Newport, Michigan, where Deputy Flicker was abducted by gangsters from Chicago. (Image courtesy the Monroe County Museum)

just two days before Flicker's abduction, Colosimo was mysteriously gunned down while leaving one of his many restaurants in Chicago. One of the most accepted theories propagated by crime historians suggests that Colosimo was unwilling to enter into the bootlegging industry, and a new generation of Chicago gangsters—namely Johnny Torrio, Al Capone, and Frankie Yale—wanted their boss out of the way to establish a profitable rumrunning organization. [270]

Whether or not these gunmen were the ones responsible for Colosimo's assassination, the Flicker incident revealed important regional developments at the beginning of the national prohibition era. Detroit and the rest of the TDW corridor was quickly becoming a staging ground for professional criminals who were building underworld connections in the area. Automobiles would play a key role in their illegal business operations throughout the entirety of the prohibition period. From the perspective of law enforcement, dry officers increasingly assumed that each vehicle speeding was a "booze car" perhaps filled with gun-toting gangsters, ultimately leading to controversial and legally questionable confrontations. And as the Chicago gangster's concern with the conditions of local roads demonstrated, the improvement and expansion of the TDW highway system greatly benefitted automobilized smugglers and criminals alike.

Dry Detroit would become a gathering place for organized bootleggers primarily because of its proximity to a legal oasis less than a mile across the Detroit River. Just as the United States came under the Volstead Act, liquor laws in Ontario loosened. Federal wartime restrictions barring Canadian citizens from having alcohol shipped directly to their homes expired on January 1, 1920.[271] Due to federal control over the liquor industry, Ontario still had dozens of breweries and distilleries fully engaged in the commercial export trade while America was boarding up its alcohol manufacturing facilities. Subsequently, the Border Cities—Windsor, Walkerville, Amherstburg, Ford City, and others—hummed with quasi-legal activity for the next decade and a half.

Newspaper reports in late 1919 indicated that many trans-border "friendships" were being "assiduously cultivated" soon after the announcement that Canada's wartime prohibition measures would be lifted in 1920. Throughout the 1920s, Americans and Canadians alike snatched up property on both sides of the Detroit River with hopes of profiting from the bootlegging business boom. Sure enough, a tidal wave of booze from across Canada flooded the Border Cities area. Reportedly 900,000 cases were shipped to Windsor and surrounding communities during the first seven months of 1920.[272] Much of that alcohol found its way across the river. By July 1920 about 1,000 cases of Ontario liquor was pouring into southeast Michigan each day.[273]

Much of the alcohol that flowed into the Border Cities in 1920 and 1921 came by truck or automobile. Although Canadians could not order directly from the nearby distilleries or breweries, legal loopholes enabled private citizens to secure their booze by other routes. With the interprovincial importation ban lifted, truckloads of beer and liquor from Quebec arrived each day at the doorsteps of Windsor area homes. An Ontario booze dealer named Jim Cooper set up an office across the river in Detroit. Taking orders from his fellow border city Canadians, Cooper "imported" Hiram Walker's Canadian Club Whiskey from the Motor City despite the fact his delivery trucks' tires never touched American pavement.[274]

In early 1920, some rumrunners opted to have their caches of booze express shipped by train, but by summer officers began to crack down on this mode of smuggling. Ontario liquor inspectors easily confiscated suspicious cargos of alcohol by simply waiting for the scheduled shipment at a designated location. In August, the *Windsor Star* reported the "liquor shipments through the express companies have fallen off to a remarkable extent" because of prohibition policing in the region.[275] Filling the bootlegging void, however, were automobiles, which had quickly become "the favorite method of transporting liquor."[276] Numerous newspaper reports show local automobilized rumrunners particularly relied upon theft—either of vehicles or crates of alcohol—to gain an advantage over enforcement officials and others working in the booze business. Villagers in neighboring Amherstburg and Maidstone pointed to the muddy tire tracks left behind by whiskey thieves as evidence of the growing use of automobiles in rumrunning. In another instance, one of Jim Cooper's liquor trucks was hijacked while delivering to a private residence in the community of Sandwich.[277]

The entire Border Cities area was quickly becoming a rumrunning and criminal paradise. Local ministers called the situation in the Border Cities a "disgrace," and claimed that Windsor was a "terrible place." They said the Canadian riverside communities were known in the United States, "especially in Detroit, as a place where liquor can be

The malt house at Hiram Walker & Sons, in Walkerville, ca 1905-1915. (Photo courtesy the Library of Congress, 2016811203)

obtained freely." After its special coverage of the criminal conditions in southwestern Ontario, the *Toronto Telegram* came to the conclusion the Border Cities were the "plague spot of Canada."[278] While Ontario's Attorney General William E. Raney variously blamed the national government, disinterested enforcers, and Windsor's horse tracks, he also alleged the problems in the area were due to the "geographic situation" that made the general vicinity "the greatest resort of gamblers and criminals on the North American continent." Almost universally prominent dry men and the local press called for an improvement in regional prohibition enforcement.[279]

Not surprisingly, one of the first rulings during the Volstead era to come out of the Windsor police court was aimed at halting automobilized smugglers transporting liquor from Quebec into Ontario. In 1920 and early 1921 it became all too common for rumrunners—from the Motor City or the Border Cities—to drive their cars through the province of Ontario to Quebec, load up their trunks and back seats, and steer their supply to the Detroit riverfront. Presiding over the case of a man allegedly moving into the area with 40 bottles in his vehicle, the local magistrate declared that under the Ontario Temperance Act it was illegal for a private citizen to act as a "common carrier" of alcohol.[280]

One incident in the spring of 1920 demonstrated both the role of autos in transporting booze and the predicament of local enforcement. During the early morning hours of St. Patrick's Day, a Windsor officer trailed an American touring car and a Canadian motor truck to a private residence. Inside he found men preparing to lower 104 crates of liquor out a second story window into the bed of the truck. With only a few automobiles assigned to the Windsor Police Department in the first few years of the 1920s, the officer instructed the men to place the alcoholic cargo into the truck, which the officer would then use to transport the violators and booze back to the station. Apparently, the policeman—who was perhaps drinking as well—pitched in to help the transfer of crates to the vehicle. With 96 crates of liquor loaded and the officer still inside the house, the men quickly jumped into the truck and into the car made their getaway. The liquor was then unloaded from the truck on to a boat waiting near the mouth of the Little River.[281]

Another policing blunder demonstrated the difficulties of enforcing prohibition amidst a growing culture of automobility in the region. Provincial officers received an anonymous tip on the night of April 5, 1920 that individuals using motorcars were planning to transport booze to the waterfront. Setting up along Matchette Road, on the outskirts of Sandwich, the officers began to halt passing cars. One driver with a female passenger, however, refused to stop his vehicle. The policemen proceeded to shoot at the vehicle and gave chase in the two police cars they had waiting in the tall grass. Their "fusillade of revolver fire" ultimately struck the driver in the neck and his wife's dress was pierced by another of the enforcer's bullets. The subsequent inspection of the auto revealed no liquor. The driver had a legitimate reason for why he failed to stop: he had been "held up at that same lonely spot" once before.[282]

Despite serious mistakes and the lack of patrol cars, police officers on the Canadian side of the Detroit River were still enforcing local dry laws. More than 7,000 cases of liquor were confiscated in Amherstburg while another 10,000 cases were seized in Windsor during the month of July 1920 alone. A multitude of newspaper articles document the prohibition enforcement activities in 1920 and 1921, many detailing extensive raids on hotels and homes and numerous arrests of drunkards and small-time bootleggers. The *Borders Cities Star* appealed to readers' sense of safety to encourage them to join in the fight against bootleggers. "High powered cars race madly up and down the border and the lives of law-abiding citizens are in continual danger. How long will this sort of thing be allowed to go on," asked the local reporter.[283]

Yet only a handful of newspaper accounts detail Borders Cities' officers halting automobilized rumrunners. With organized logistics and mechanical advantage, it is clear why these professionals were not frequently caught. Automobiles with hidden caches under the driver's seat were believed to be crossing the border at will aboard motorcar ferries operating around Windsor. An investigative reporter for the *Toledo Telegram* closely followed local bootleggers and revealed some of their tactics to avoid detection. The motorized smugglers employed a "systems of signals" and hired lookouts who helped them "baffle even an alert or well-organized police force."[284] Colored t-shirts on roadside clothes lines indicated whether officers were in the vicinity. Both day and night motorized trucks transported alcoholic supplies from Border Cities' depots and storehouses to the riverfront.[285]

To gain ground on these booze smugglers, Ontario's Attorney General Raney increased the number of provincial liquor inspectors working in Essex County and gave them the authority to hire as "many men as they needed to fight the liquor traffic." Their most noteworthy hire was a local Method minister known as the "fighting parson," J.O.L Spracklin. A fervent dry, Spracklin made headlines when he reported in the summer of 1920 that a Sandwich roadhouse was clearly violating the Ontario Temperance Act. Spracklin counted 25 to 30 automobiles parked outside and taxi after taxi dropping off Americans looking to drink. Visitors stumbled out of the hotel speakeasy in a drunken stupor. Sitting on the porch of the roadhouse was the 80-year-old village police chief, whose inaction spoke volumes to Spracklin. "There is a flagrant disregard for the law and so far, the police have made no effective efforts to cope with the situation," clamored the Methodist minister.[286]

Spracklin quickly wore out his welcome. Just a few months into the job, the prohibitionist pastor shot and killed the owner of the Sandwich roadhouse he staked out just months before. Though acquitted on evidence that he acted in self-defense, Spracklin was dismissed from his position as a local liquor agent. Even before this notorious incident,

Spracklin's dealings with suspected smugglers placed the spotlight on the minister. He and his team of "special" investigators frequently disregarded Canadian law and policing best practices, including when it came to motor vehicle stops. Revealing his bias against other Christian denominations, Spracklin was known to set up illegal checkpoints after the release of Mass at a local Catholic Church. Without warrants or probable cause, the minister and his "specials" searched cars up and down, sometimes accepting handsome bribes from actual rumrunners to supplement their enforcement incomes. Among Spracklin's hired men, Stanley and William Hallam were considered to be the most corrupt. These gun-wielding brothers infamously preyed upon cab drivers in the Border Cities, pulling them over without probable cause and demanding pay-offs to ensure avoiding court time, fees, or worse. They too were dismissed from their posts a week before Spracklin's shooting.[287]

If law enforcement could not stop automobilized bootleggers, local drys hoped that the successful passage of a provincial referendum would do the trick. On April 18, 1921, Ontario residents overwhelmingly decided in favor of prohibiting the importation of liquor in the province, which one area newspaper predicted would effectively halt "the pilots of illicit motor-car cargoes." Just a few months later, Cecil Smith, a former taxi driver turned professional rumrunner, was sentenced to five years in prison for attempting to bribe an officer as Smith's men illegally transferred 750 cases of liquor from a freight car into five touring cars and seven trucks. It was perhaps the greatest prohibition victory for Border Cities law enforcement, especially considering that Smith admitted to paying $96,000 worth of local bootleggers' fines.[288]

Smith's candid testimony, however, pointed to the reality of rumrunning along the Detroit River. The bootlegger claimed he made his money not by selling booze on Canadian soil but by facilitating the movement of liquor "in large quantities to the United States." Distilleries and breweries operating in the Border Cities continued to churn out product for the lucrative export trade, which was handled by third party export companies positioned along the riverfront. One Toronto newspaper reporter covering the Windsor area declared international bootlegging "had been raised to the dignity of a profession." By the end of 1921, it was estimated that 1,000 cases of intoxicants were shipped daily across the river into Michigan.[289]

The provincial government once again attempted to dam the flow of booze pouring through the Border Cities with new legislation and legally questionable seizures. In early August 1921, liquor agents confiscated 100 cartons of beer being transported by a brewery truck to the export docks in Sandwich, from where it was supposed to be shipped across the river to residents in Wyandotte, Michigan. In this landmark test case, a Windsor court ruled it could "not prevent the export of liquor from Ontario to any other country," even to the United States which had its own set of prohibition laws.[290] The agents had to relinquish the seized goods and the local brewery proceeded with the shipment through an export company. Just a few days after the ruling, the *Border Cities Star* reported that "truck load after truck load" was being delivered daily to the docks in Walkerville and Sandwich. In a last ditch effort to stymie the transportation of beer and liquor to the riverfront, provincial legislators passed a bill in June 1922 that prohibited the transportation of alcohol on Ontario's public highways, effectively targeting the use of trucks and automobiles. Subsequent seizures by local police were later invalidated by the local courts system and the Liquor Transportation Bill was ultimately struck down as "an encroachment upon the jurisdiction of the Federal Government."[291]

[269] May 12, 1920; "Four Auto Gunmen Seize Deputy Sheriff and Take Him Away," *Monroe Evening News*, May 13, 1920; "Deputy is Safe: Taken to Detroit and Released After Gun Was Unloaded," *Monroe Evening News*, May 13, 1920; "Seek to Head off Rum Smugglers," *Toledo News-Bee*, May 13, 1920; "Officer Kidnapped by Rum Runners," *Detroit Free Press*, May 14, 1920.

[270] "Colosimo Slain; Seek Ex-Wife, Just Returned," *Chicago Tribune*, May 12, 1920; "Captor of Cop May Be Slayers," *Toledo News-Bee*, May 14, 1920; John Binder, *Al Capone's Beer Wars: A Complete History of Organized Crime in Chicago During Prohibition* (Amherst, New York: Prometheus Books, 2017), 60-61.

[271]

[272] "Windsor Gulps in Anticipation," *Detroit Free Press*, December 22, 1919; "4,000 Newcomers Settle in Windsor," *Detroit Free Press*, October 29, 1919; "Demand Increases for Lakefront Sites," *Detroit Free Press*, August 7, 1927.

[273] "Prohibition in Ontario, 1919-1923," *Ontario Historical Society*, 1972, 118; Philip Mason, *Rum-Running and the Roaring Twenties: Prohibition on the Michigan-Ontario Waterway*, (Detroit: Wayne State University, 1995), 38.

[274] Marty Gervais, *The Rumrunners: A Prohibition Scrapbook* (Biblioasis: Emeryville, Canada, 2009), 65-66; Philip Mason, *Rum-Running and the Roaring Twenties: Prohibition on the Michigan-Ontario Waterway*, (Detroit: Wayne State University, 1995), 37-38.

[275] "Two Shipments of Liquor Are Ordered Seized" *Border Cities Star*, August 6, 1920.

[276] "Says Rainey Quite Within His Rights," *Border Cities Star*, August 6, 1920.

[277] "Unique Case; Liquor Taken by Inspector," *Border Cities Star*, July 10, 1920; "Express Agent Dismissed on Liquor Charges," *Border Cities Star*, June 15, 1920; "Burg Resident Loses Liquor," *Border Cities Star*, November 20, 1920; "Officers Find Liquor Hidden in Some Hay," *Border Cities Star*, June 23, 1920; "Border Cellars Banned to Thirsty Detroiters," *Border Cities Star*, January 14, 1920. For other related articles see: "Truck Driver Jailed and Fined $1,000," *Border Cities Star*, August 6, 1920; "Steals Auto Truck to Smuggle Liquor," *Border Cities Star*, January 6, 1920; "Two are Freed on Charge of Theft of Load of Whiskey," *Border Cities Star*, January 20, 1921; "Halts Motor Cars; Charges Will be Laid," *Border Cities Star*, June 15, 1921; "Nine Liquor Bandits Fire Thirty Shots," *Border Cities Star*, June 1, 1921.

[278] "Toronto Paper Scores Rum-runnning on Essex Border and Elsewhere," *Border Cities Star*, June 19, 1920.

[279] "Writs Claiming Damages to be Issued as a Result of Liquor Traffic Charges," *Border Cities Star*, June 23, 1920; "Border Bootlegging is Talk of Land; 'Plague Spot' One Writer Says," *Border Cities Star*, July 10, 1920; "Raney Rap Local Police, Federal Gov't," *Border Cities Star*, August 6, 1920.

[280] "May Not Transport Liquor Personally, Is Ruling of Court," *Windsor Star*, March 22, 1920.

[281] Philip Mason, *Rum-Running and the Roaring Twenties: Prohibition on the Michigan-Ontario Waterway*, (Detroit: Wayne State University, 1995), 38; Marty Gervais, *The Border Police: One Hundred and Twenty-Five Years of Policing in Windsor* (Watrerloo, Ontario: Penumbra Press, 1992), 41, 46.

[282] "Probe Into Shooting of Local Man by Police is Started Before Judge," *Border Cities Star*, June 2, 1920.

[283] "Prohibition in Ontario, 1919-1923," *Ontario Historical Society*, 1972, 118; "Toronto Paper Scores Rum-runnning on Essex Border and Elsewhere," *Border Cities Star*, June 19, 1920.

[284] "Toronto Paper Scores Rum-running on Essex Border and Elsewhere," *Border Cities Star*, June 19, 1920

[285] "Prohibition in Ontario, 1919-1923," *Ontario Historical Society*, 1972, 118; "Toronto Paper Scores Rum-running on Essex Border and Elsewhere," *Border Cities Star*, June 19, 1920; "Border Bootlegging is Talk of Land; 'Plague Spot' One Writer Says," *Border Cities Star*, July 10, 1920.

[286] Gerry Hallowell, "Prohibition in Ontario, 1919-1923," *Ontario Historical Society*, 1972, 120-121.

[287] Patrick Brode, *Dying for a Drink: How a Prohibition Preacher Got Away with Murder* (Biblioasis: Windsor, Ontario, 2018), 85, 96 101, 107; "Hallam Brothers are Dismissed by Pastor-Inspector," *Border Cities Star,* October 23, 1920.

[288] "Says He Paid $96,000 to the Government," *Borders Cities Star*, October 13, 1921; Gerry Hallowell "Prohibition in Ontario, 1919-1923," *Ontario Historical Society*, 1972, 79, 91.

[289] "Says He Paid $96,000 to the Government," *Borders Cities Star*, October 13, 1921; Patrick Brode, *Dying for a Drink: How a Prohibition Preacher Got Away with Murder* (Biblioasis: Windsor, Ontario, 2018).

[290] "Brewery Can Ship Beer to U.S. Markets," *Border Cities Star*, August 10, 1921.

[291] "Flow of Canadian Beer to American Points Unchecked," *Border Cities Star*; August 13, 1921; "Unlawful to Utilize Truck Since Tuesday," *Border Cities Star*, June 15, 1922; "No Trucking Law Blocked by Resolution," *Border Cities Star*, June 16, 1922; "Hydro Lines Permitted to Deliver Beer," *Border Cities Star*, June 23, 1922; "Ontario to Prevent Leakage of Liquor," *Border Cities Star*, July 12, 1922; "Judge Coughlin Kills Conviction Against Brewery," *Border Cities Star*, January 9, 1923.

CHAPTER 13
Henry Ford's Battle Against Booze

With Canadian dry agents' hands tied, booze continued to pour over the international border for the remainder of the decade. America's "Prohibition Navy," operating on the Detroit River and Lake Erie, was just as ineffective. Detroit historian Philip Mason's *Rum-Running and the Roaring Twenties* points out that professional rumrunners clearly possessed the advantage on the waterways throughout the dry era. Motor-savvy smugglers were, as one Detroit Police Commissioner admitted, "running circles around" their government-issued vessels. One federal analysis in 1928 indicated that waterborne agents captured only five percent of the alcohol leaving Border Cities' docks. The remaining 95 percent usually landed successfully ashore in Michigan or Ohio.[292]

Profitable rumrunning rings, however, were not satisfied with just getting their cargo ashore. Successful smugglers needed reliable automobiles, accessible storage facilities, and organized logistics in order to distribute cases of booze quickly and discreetly to local speakeasies, private citizens, and other professional distributors. Without a doubt, the motorcar was *the* primary component of large-scale bootlegging and all aspects of this criminal enterprise were oriented around it. James R. Davis, the Federal Prohibition Director of Michigan, plainly stated in a 1925 interview that "practically all of the transportation of liquor is by automobile."[293] Nonetheless, trucks and flivvers not only waited at the shoreline to be loaded up and driven away but they also served as decoys. Rumrunners admitted to the *Detroit Free Press* that accomplices lined their vehicles on the coastline and intermittently flashed their headlights as if they were sending signals to waterborne smugglers. Dry agents descended upon these faulty locations as the actual rumrunners transferred their cargoes of booze from vessel to vehicle at another spot along the river. Automobilized bootleggers openly bragged about their ability to load fifteen to twenty crates of liquor in a minute.[294]

Nevertheless, other area smugglers did not have to worry about how quickly they loaded up crates of beer or whiskey. A 1926 raid of a riverside residence in Ecorse, Michigan revealed a rumrunner's dream home that apparently had been in use since the first years of the Volstead era. Besides having a massive storage area for alcohol, the house had a boat well with direct access to the Detroit River. The boathouse possessed a "veritable maze of doors and series of passages" which secretly led to another building on the property that "was used as a loading station for the motor trucks by which the liquor was distributed."[295]

Boating bootleggers could also rely upon the advanced infrastructure of the TDW corridor. Unlike other areas in the Midwest, the region possessed an elaborate road system that frequently came within a few hundred feet of the water. Some rumrunners preferred to land their watercraft in the bayous and marshlands of Monroe County. Not only was the county's shore thinly populated and lacking in enforcement officials, these isolated spots were also "easily accessible to main highways."[296]

From these landing spots along the Detroit River or Lake Erie, much of the booze "rolled westward on wheels" to Chicago, where Al Capone and others made immense profits from their ties with Detroit-area smugglers who supplied them Canadian liquor and beer. Yet, a significant portion of the smugglers' truckloads headed north and south, to Detroit, Toledo, and beyond. Estimates of the number of blind pigs operating in Detroit ranged wildly from 3,000 to 15,000 in the first five years of national prohibition. Regardless of the actual number, Motor City speakeasies were fully dependent on automobilized bootleggers for their supply.[297] Sixty miles to the south, in Toledo, Federal Prohibition agent Daniel Crane noted that due to its relative proximity to Canada and local rumrunners' ready access to "fast autos and motor trucks," Toledo had become a hub for booze smuggling. Crane noted the Glass City was "beautifully placed...to send caravans of illicit cheer to arid wastes of Ohio."[298] Editorials in northwest Ohio newspapers simultaneously

A photojournalist for the *Detroit News* hid in a coal elevator to snap this photo of rumrunners loading their cars at the foot of Riopelle Street near downtown Detroit. (Photo courtesy Wayne State University, Walter P. Reuther Library)

condemned the "flow of bootleg poison" into Toledo and implored the city's residents to demand better enforcement of prohibition.[299]

A prominent resident in the suburban Detroit area also demanded better enforcement of dry laws in the early 1920s. Industrialist Henry Ford was at first confident that prohibition would bring order to both his factories and human society as a whole. During the first year of the Michigan state ban on alcohol, Ford shared workplace statistics with the Anti-Saloon League (ASL), which in turn published them in its nationally syndicated *American Issue*. "On the last Monday in April, 2,620 [Ford factory] men were absent from work because of Saturday night drinking," reported the June 1918 edition of the *American Issue*.[300] Nevertheless, significantly fewer workers were skipping work once the state prohibition began enforcement in May. The Ford Motor Company happily reported to the ASL that absenteeism had been reduced to 1,618 for the first Monday of May and further diminished to 1,536 the following Monday. Ford, in a 1919 interview with the *Cleveland Plain Dealer*, confidently predicted the "day is almost at hand when mankind will nevermore drink intoxicants."[301] *The Dearborn Independent* and *The Ford Times*—a pair of publications owned by Henry Ford—published numerous articles advocating the dry cause during the early years of prohibition.[302]

By 1922, it was increasingly clear to the automobile magnate that prohibition was not being effectively enforced in the vicinity of his factories, as illustrated by existing sources from within the Ford Motor Company's office of the era. In particular, one 1922 report written by a local emergency doctor was forwarded by Ford's office to Roy Haynes, the Federal Prohibition Commissioner. The doctor described how a Ford foundry sweeper named Hyman Shapiro died in his care on August 26. Shapiro, suffering from a "drunken stupor," was found in a ditch during the early hours of a workday by another Ford employee who, in turn, dropped him off near the foundry. After he was brought to the factory's first aid station, Shapiro was then transferred to the local hospital where he fell into an unconscious state. The foundry sweeper was pronounced dead later that morning and the cause was determined to be "acute alcoholism." Shaprio left behind a wife and two children, one of them being recently adopted.[303]

In another letter to Haynes' office, Ford's personal secretary, Ernest G. Liebold, claimed enforcement of the Volstead Act in the Detroit metro area was a "farce." Stills and rumrunners were operating within a "stone's throw" of the company's River Rouge factory gates and gallons of moonshine was being regularly smuggled into the automotive plant. Most alarmingly, Liebold noted, was a nearby restaurant that was selling intoxicating beverages in "open view," causing several drunk workers to be sent home early each day. To say the least, Ford Motor Company hoped that policing of the nation's dry laws would be taken more seriously.[304]

At the same time, Ford began to take enforcement of prohibition into his own hands. Speaking on behalf of his company, the famous industrialist proclaimed that political shenanigans had interfered with the effectiveness of the Eighteenth Amendment, which Ford called a "fundamental law of this country." Nevertheless, the carmaker was undeterred, stating as "far as our organization is concerned, it's going to be enforced to the letter." Ford immediately ordered his supervisors to administer a sniffing test of their workers on every shift. If an employee was found to have the "odor of intoxicants" on his breath they would be immediately fired. Ford reportedly justified this stern punishment by stating "beer, wine, and liquor never did anybody any good—and they have caused incalculable suffering and misery in the world."[305]

Magazines throughout the country widely disseminated news of Ford's stern policy. One business owner in North Carolina, after reading about the anti-alcohol measures taken by the Ford Motor Company, felt compelled to pen a laudatory letter commending the automotive giant. "We wish to express to you our hearty approval and endorsement of the stand you have taken, which we hope will be a signal for other manufacturers," stated the cotton mill executive. The letter also shared the businessman's views on prohibition, claiming "one of the greatest hindrances to the effective enforcement of the Eighteenth Amendment is that it is so often regarded as having been enacted so as to apply only to the laboring man…In the moulding of public opinion and sentiment on any great subject, we believe that the example should be set and the way be shown from the top instead of the bottom…" At the very least, Henry Ford was considered a leading industrial advocate for bringing about a dry American work environment.[306]

Ford also utilized private investigators to gather information about the bootlegging underworld just outside his factory gates and in neighboring communities. In a letter to the Federal Prohibition office, Liebold noted that Ford Motor Company hired a newspaper reporter to "make a survey" of all the stills and moonshiners in operation near their automotive plants.[307] Another revealing November 1922 letter sent to

Members of the Monroe County Sheriff's department show off the spoils from numerous raids in 1922. (Photo courtesy the Monroe County Museum)

Liebold by a man named George Rounds documents his surveillance of Ecorse, a Downriver town just ten miles from Detroit. Rounds surmised after a week of undercover work that Ecorse was "owned and run by bootleggers" and was primarily responsible for the influx of booze in the region.[308] Saloons and blind pigs openly operated in the riverside hamlet as drunken parties imbibed until the early hours of the morning. It was a

Officers discovered this 30-foot tall still inside a fake house in Monroe. The giant still was reassembled at the Rockwood State Police Post for the public to see. (Photo courtesy Rockwood Area Historical Museum)

common sight, according to Rounds, for the intoxicated to use the "street as a toilet" and for inebriated women to be carried out of random houses and establishments. He also took special note of the continuous arrival of rumrunning boaters from Canada and the numerous automobiles that hauled off the illegal cargo over land. Rounds concluded that what he witnessed in Ecorse was just a "sample of the activities and conditions which our employees and their families are up against."[309] Henry Ford's office would later relay this information to Commissioner Haynes, resulting in closer cooperation between Ford Motor and the country's leading dry agents.[310]

With Henry Ford complaining about enforcement conditions around his factories and national journalists calling the entire TDW corridor a "booze runner's fairyland," American prohibition authorities felt compelled to clean up rumrunning in the area.[311] Commissioner Haynes decided to first send in his star undercover investigator Isidore "Izzy" Einstein, either in late 1922 or early 1923. Einstein claimed that it was indeed the complaints of "motor companies" who were experiencing "more and more mechanics reporting for work in a condition of hangover" that convinced Haynes to station him in the metro Detroit area. Dressed as an unemployed factory worker, Einstein hovered around automobile plants and made friends with homeless drunkards on the streets. Izzy frequented numerous blind pigs and clubs in Detroit and nearby Hamtramck where he secretly gathered liquid evidence.[312]

While Einstein engaged in the undercover work, highly publicized "drives," "blockades," and "campaigns" were conducted by federal and state forces to root out speakeasies and the waterborne traffic supplying them.[313] Coordinated raids in Detroit, Hamtramck, Toledo, Ecorse, and other downriver towns made newspaper headlines in 1922, 1923, and 1925. Nearly 50 places were served warrants and padlocked in the Motor City alone in June 1923.[314] Despite their vigorous efforts, enforcement officials quickly realized they also had to confront the automobilized nature of regional smuggling. Increasingly equipped with their own motorcycles and vehicles, dry agents descended upon locations along the Detroit River in Ecorse and neighboring Wyandotte to halt rumrunner's trucks in their tracks, confiscating the motorcars that were directly involved in these illegal endeavors.[315]

At first, local enforcement efforts seemed to be paying off. Newspaper reporters indicated the regional bootlegging industry was significantly hampered, especially in communities like Ecorse and Hamtramck.[316] In fact, due to increased policing in the Detroit metro area, some Toledo rumrunners—rather than risk being arrested—opted to drive 2,800 miles to and from Savannah, Georgia to supply their customers. The "long haul" was still worth it. Veteran smugglers paid $1,500 for their liquor but later sold their illegal cargo for $4,200 in the Glass City.[317] Dry agents working in the area, however, knew that the proverbial plug would not hold long. Though he expressed some optimism about his officers' efforts, E.C. Yellowely, a federal prohibition administrator who spent considerable time in the Motor City, noted that rumrunning conditions were "not much improved" since the drive started. He also admitted while other cities like New York, Pittsburgh, and Cincinnati were "doing splendidly," Detroit was "not doing so well."[318]

---

[292] Philip Mason, *Rum-Running and the Roaring Twenties: Prohibition on the Michigan-Ontario Waterway*, (Detroit: Wayne State University, 1995), 104-106.

[293] "Wants Wider Liquor Search," *Detroit Free Press*, February 22, 1925.

[294] "Rum-Runners, Agents Play 'Hide and Seek,'" *Detroit Free Press*, June 18, 1929.

[295] "Liquor Vaults Yields $100,000 Loot in Raid," *Detroit Free Press*, November 4, 1926.

[296] "Monroe Helpless to Stem Rum Tide," *Detroit Free Press*, October 9, 1927.

[297] "Monroe Helpless to Stem Rum Tide," *Detroit Free Press*, October 9, 1927; "Croul Flays Rum Crusade," *Detroit Free Press*, December 25, 1923; "Police Raid 51 Places in Huge Vice Roundup," *Detroit Free Press*, March 17, 1924; "15,000 Blind Pigs in Detroit, Police Official Declares," *Port Huron Times Herald*, February 14, 1925; "Catch a Bootlegger? 'Tell Us How Judge," *Detroit Free Press*, August 30, 1923.

[298] "Toledo is Boon for Rum Trade," *Detroit Free Press*, January 15, 1922.

[299] "The Poison Flood," *Toledo News-Bee*, January 20, 1922.

[300] "Detroit Rises in Testimonial," *American Issue,* June 15, 1918; "The Milk Bottle and a Clear Head in Detroit Have a 75 Day Demonstration" *American Issue,* August 17,1918.

[301] "Henry Ford Says He Loves Alcohol," *Cleveland Plain Dealer*, June 2, 1919.

[302] "The Story of a Reform", *Dearborn Independent*, February 15, 1919; "To Finish the Saloon", *Dearborn Independent,* January 25, 1919; "The Dry and Wet Vote" *Dearborn Independent,* April 19, 1919; "Add Thirty Days," *Dearborn Independent,* February 13, 1919; "The Saloon and Chemicalized Booze are Dead", *Dearborn Independent,* December 10, 1921. "Ridiculing Prohibition", *Dearborn Independent,* January 21, 1922;" Do Not be Deceived," *Ford Times,* October 5, 1923.

[303] B.D Campbell to E.G. Liebold, September 15, 1922, Box 106, Accession 285, Ford Motor Company Archives, Dearborn Michigan.

[304] E.G. Liebold to Roy A. Haynes, September 23, 1922, Box 106, Accession 285, Ford Motor Company Archives, Dearborn Michigan.

[305] "No Breath of Rum in the Ford Works", *Literary Digest* vol. 74, September 30, 1922, 12-13.

[306] "Henry Ford Points the Way to Other Leaders in Industry in Prohibition of Intoxicants in His Plant" Manufacturers Record, vol. 82, no. 2, December 7, 1922, 82-83; Lawrence S. Holt to Henry Ford, December 11, 1922, Box 106, Accession 285, Ford Motor Company Archives, Dearborn Michigan.

[307] Liebold to Haynes, September 23, 1922, Box 91, Accession 285, Ford Motor Company Archives, Dearborn, Michigan.

[308] Rounds to Liebold, November 13, 1922, Box 91, Accession 285, Ford Motor Company Archives, Dearborn Michigan.

[309] Ibid.

[310] Dec 4 1922 Liebold to Haynes, December 20, 1922, Box 91, Accession 285, Ford Motor Company Archives, Dearborn Michigan.

[311] "2 Years' Prohibition Cuts Drinking 60 P.C.," *New York Herald*, January 8, 1922.

[312] Izzy Einstein, *Prohibition Agent No. 1,* (New York: Frederick A. Stokes Co., 1932), 202-214.

[313] "Izzy and Moe Tips Start Detroit Raid," *New York Times*, June 15, 1923; "3 Are Nabbed, $1,000 Liquor Taken in Raid," *Detroit Free Press* December 8, 1923;; "River Patrol Nabs Rum Boat," *Detroit Free Press*, June 16, 1923; "Fool Dry Navy Caught Ashore."

[314] "Two Year Dry Fight Too Short to Decide Prohibition's Future," *The Ogden Standard-Examiner*, February 19, 1922; "4 Ecorse Rum Caches Raided," Detroit Free Press, March 25, 1922; "Ecorse Not Same Town Since Davis Butted In," Detroit Free Press, May 15, 1922; "Dry Agents Drive Cause Bootleggers to Shift Base," Lansing State Journal, June 23, 1923; "4 Ecorse Rum Caches Raided," Detroit Free Press, March 25, 1922; "3 Are Nabbed, $1,000 Liquor Taken in Raid," Detroit Free Press December 8, 1923; "Booze Sleuths Mop Up Here; 15 Taken in Raids," *Toledo News-Bee*, July 10, 1925; "Drys Padlock 50 Oases Here in Liquor War," Detroit Free Press, June 15, 1923; "Enlarged Dry Army is Here" *Detroit Free Press*, June 17, 1923.

[315] "Fool Dry Navy Caught Ashore," *Detroit Free Press*, June 20, 1923; "Rum Runners Fight Officers, Hit Bystander," *Detroit Free Press*, June 27, 1923.

[316] "Ecorse Not Same Town Since Davis Butted In," *Detroit Free Press*, May 15, 1922; "Patrol Hurts Bootleg Trade," *Detroit Free Press*, June 26, 1923.

[317] "Bootleggers Meet Problem of Long Haul from Gulf Ports," *Toledo News-Bee*, September 14, 1922.

[318] "Rum Laden Car; No Warrant, No Case," *Detroit Free Press*, June 15, 1923; "Croul Flays Rum Crusade," *Detroit Free Press*, December 25, 1923; "Rum Padlock Threatens 36," *Detroit Free Press*, June 16, 1923.

CHAPTER 14
Motor Vehicle Exception: Dry Enforcement Conundrum on the TDW Corridor

The proximity of Canada was the main reason it was so difficult to halt the flow of booze on the TDW corridor in the early and mid-1920s. Yet, another important development preventing progress against automobilized rumrunners was the fact that it was not yet firmly established—legally or ethically—how enforcement officials should confront motorists suspected of active illegal endeavors.

Local dry leaders, including Henry Ford and Ohio's president of the Women's Christian Temperance Union, advocated for the use of guns and military tactics when enforcing prohibition. However, when local officers utilized deadly force they were frequently criticized by local citizens, sued for damages, or even arrested.[319] The case of a constable operating near Toledo in late 1923 exemplified such a predicament. William Frazier used his automobile to block a public highway north of the Glass City and shot eleven rounds towards a suspected bootlegging vehicle that failed to stop. The oncoming car smashed into the officer's car, causing a local man to fly through the windshield and sustain serious injuries. The pair of men in the vehicle—in which no alcohol was found—claimed they were afraid of being held up by highwaymen. Constable Frazier was arrested and faced a lawsuit totaling $11,000.[320]

Warrantless apprehensions of rumrunners and seizures of their booze-filled vehicles were often scrutinized. Without any legal precedent affirming that dry agents could use probable cause to arrest motorists suspected of bootlegging, officers were routinely taken to court for improper prohibition policing when automobiles were involved. For example, an Ecorse smuggler was freed of all dry charges in the summer of 1923 despite the fact he was caught transporting a large load of liquor from a location notorious for its bootlegging activities. Though the arresting officer claimed he saw cases of liquor in the backseat, such a stop was ruled impermissible without a warrant.[321] A similar instance just a few months later allowed a Toledo rumrunner to walk free despite having 100 gallons of "white mule" in tow. At first, the accused man pleaded guilty but his attorney wittingly advised him to challenge the lack of "proper papers when he was arrested."[322] To avoid legal troubles and to ensure the evidence was not driven away, dry agents on the TDW corridor sometimes had to act quick to obtain a search warrant when dealing with cars full of liquor.[323]

A questionable traffic stop in western Michigan two years earlier would ultimately decide the legal debte over warrantless searches of vehicles. On December 15, 1921, federal agents stationed on a public highway connecting Grand Rapids to Detroit recognized an Oldsmobile Roadster traveling westbound. It was that of a gang of rumrunners they had tried unsuccessfully to infiltrate a few months earlier. Without search warrants, the officers decided to pull the vehicle over anyhow and search for illegal cargo. Sure enough, 68 bottles of scotch and gin were hidden in the upholstery of the backseat. The rumrunners were convicted in lower courts, but their appeal finally reached the U.S. Supreme Court on March 2, 1925. By a 7-2 decision, the court affirmed in Carroll v. United States that the agents' search and seizure was constitutional.[324] Not only was the "search not malicious or without probable cause," according to the majority opinion penned by former president William Howard Taft, but it was "not practical to secure a search warrant, because the vehicle can be quickly moved out of the locality or jurisdiction where the warrant must be sought." This landmark decision not only provided greater legal freedom for prohibition enforcers on the TDW corridor

Bottles of liquor that had been hidden in the false bottom of a truck. (Photo courtesy Michigan State University)

and around the country to halt suspected rumrunning automobiles, but it established the "motor vehicle exception" to the Fourth Amendment that still influences traffic stops today.[325]

Even with this legal hurdle cleared, rumrunners continued to gum up local court systems with appeals that compelled arresting officers to defend their reasons for halting vehicles transporting alcohol. Monroe County Circuit Court records reveal that bootleggers' defense attorneys in the mid-1920s regularly targeted whether sheriff deputies or state troopers truly possessed probable cause or proper jurisdiction to search their defendant's automobiles.

In one such case, lawyers for an automobilized rumrunner called into question whether state police could search a vehicle after stopping it for a license plate violation and allegedly smelling moonshine upon approaching the car.[326] Another case involved whether troopers could use a motorist's keys to seize champagne and whiskey after allegedly witnessing the trunk of the bootlegger's Chevrolet couple fly open and close in one motion.[327] Other controversial cases centered around whether law enforcement had the authority in certain locations to seize booze. One such rumrunning case was ultimately dismissed after officers crossed over into Ohio to stop a vehicle for speeding in southern Monroe County, ultimately finding 17 crates of Canadian beer in the backseat but outside of their legal jurisdiction.[328] Yet another case was dependent upon whether a state trooper had observed the loading of alcohol into an automobile on a privately-owned road.[329]

Dry agents became bolder in their efforts to combat automobiles transporting booze, but smugglers on the TDW corridor were still running rampant in the mid to late 1920s. In the midst of the crackdown on Ecorse, one local rumrunner told an Associated Press journalist that he had driven 40,000 miles back and forth from the Detroit River to Chicago with no interference from enforcers on the TDW corridor.[330] Indeed, prohibition campaigns or drives in the region were only temporary and rarely could their impact be felt beyond the specific communities that were targeted. During regular enforcement times only a "little body" of state troopers and another 24 to 30 men from the federal government were actively patrolling the 70 mile shoreline from Detroit to Toledo during a given shift. During a 1927 inspection of enforcement practices, the assistant attorney general stated that the Detroit River "district is woefully short-handed in regard to prohibition agents." Crafty smugglers would operate at full tilt and the culture of automobility underpinned their continued success. [331]

Some historians point to the fact that bootleggers' successes were largely due to their ownership of superior cars. So-called Whiskey Sixes—automobiles that were outfitted with six cylinder engines and could travel at least 60 miles an hour—gave wealthier rumrunners a significant advantage. However, many local police departments also upgraded during the prohibition period. In 1921, the Toledo Police

A Toledo Police Department Overland service car in Toledo's warehouse district, ca 1918. (Photo courtesy the Toledo-Lucas County Public Library, Images in Time)

discarded their seven "tin can" Fords and purchased six Marmon Speedsters.[332] Capable of reaching 82 miles per hour, these new cars were able to compete with most high-powered rumrunning vehicles on the road. In 1925, Monroe's police department bought a new vehicle reportedly "equipped with balloon tires and capable of 70 miles an hour." No longer on horseback, state troopers working along the Detroit River arrived quickly to loading sites on their new motorcycles.[333]

When rumrunners in powerful cars attempted to speed away, dry agents in the region were almost always able to catch up and apprehend the suspects. In turn, this resulted in the seizure of hundreds of bootlegging automobiles on the TDW corridor, especially in the metro area of the Motor City. In 1924, before the Carroll v. United States decision, just 21 automobiles and trucks were confiscated in Detroit. During a ten-month period three years later, over 300 motorcars were

A pair of Toledo police officers with their new, faster, squad car, ca 1930. (Photo courtesy the Toledo-Lucas County Public Library, Images in Time)

seized by authorities working in the Detroit region. Not surprisingly, officers patrolling the Detroit River border were fully "motorized," using close to 300 autos that had been previously driven by rumrunners. [334]

Yet, confiscating smugglers' vehicles did not always have the intended effect. In 1925, James Sprott, the Detroit Police Department's Assistant Superintendent, told the *Detroit Free Press* it was of little use to seize a first-time offender's car.[335] Frequently these men would just pay a fine and be back "at the old game in another boat or auto in a few hours." Sprott claimed the "principals" funding these drivers immediately "put the seizure of his vehicle down to profit and loss and gave him another."[336]

In Toledo, dry enforcers apparently had issues with a local garage they subcontracted to tow seized motorcars. The proprietor of the Kirk Garage Company and three of their mechanics confessed to stealing cases of booze left from confiscated cars stored in their facility.[337] To raise funds for local prohibition enforcement efforts, confiscated vehicles were sometimes sold to at public auctions in Detroit and Toledo. At one auction in Detroit, the sale of eight seized cars fetched $3,765 for federal dry agents. Three of the cars, however, were bought back by their rumrunning owners. Newspaper reports also indicated that officers sometimes failed to destroy hidden liquor tanks or concealed cavities in the car prior to selling them.[338]

Local rumrunners attempted to use their motorcar expertise and the surrounding automobile culture to transport booze on the TDW corridor. In one of its several prohibition-era exposes of bootlegging around Detroit, the *New York Times* reported there was "no small number of those who make a living in the motor car and its allied trades" significantly adding to their middle-class salaries by bootlegging on the side.[339] The police blotters in local newspapers documented how numerous automobile mechanics, car salesman, tire retailers, and taxi drivers were arrested transporting booze, but many others undoubtedly were never caught.

A pair of traffic stops beyond the TDW corridor revealed how local tinkerers had modified their motorcars to avoid capture or detection. In nearby Ypsilanti, a Detroit rumrunner was pulled over with "a specially constructed car, built to conceal a large number of bottles."[340] In the downriver town of Trenton, a motorcycle cop was trailing an automobile suspected of hauling alcohol. Suddenly the vehicle spewed out a "cloud of poisonous gas," causing the motorcycle cop to career off the road. A manhunt ensued and the car was located several days later near the Motor City. The driver happened to be a Detroiter and his vehicle was equipped with a "small tank...under the floor of the car with an outlet in the exhaust pipe."[341] An automobile outfitted with a similar exhaust system was confiscated in Monroe County that same year. Police further reported rumrunning vehicles emitting "sharp metallic objects" to puncture the tires of cars in pursuit. The mechanical minds of the area even reengineered boat motors and their exhaust systems with automobile mufflers to sneak across the Detroit River with Canadian beer.[342]

Local dry law enforcers frequently caught smugglers trying to take advantage of some of the more unique aspects of automobility in their attempts to blend in with the traveling masses. As more women took the wheel in the 1920s, they were also increasingly tasked with transporting loads of booze along the TDW corridor, as indicated by arrest reports. Apparently, it was not until 1928 that the so-called "flapper rumrunner" ploy was raised to a level of concern at the federal prohibition office in Washington D.C. Dry agents working on the TDW corridor, however, were already well aware of the growing presence of women steering booze through the region, and local newspapers were calling it a "new social problem" as early as 1923.[343] State troopers stationed in Monroe County consistently caught Toledo and Detroit women hauling gallons of liquor in the mid-1920s. Toledo's "Rum Queen," Ada Biddle, was arrested in the summer of 1928 for orchestrating a vast smuggling ring just outside the Glass City.[344] Younger and older populations became more accustomed to driving, and soon they too were transporting alcohol in the area. Grandmothers, teenage boys, and young ladies were apprehended smuggling booze in their respective vehicles.[345]

While businesses and industries were using motorcars to grow their businesses, automobilized bootleggers also took advantage of this trend to avoid detection. It did not always work, as indicated by intermittent newspaper accounts detailing their capture while engaging in deceptive

A Prohibition agent stands in a flatbed of confiscated alcohol at the Trumbull Street Police Station on Detroit's West Side. (Photo courtesy Wayne State University, Walter P. Reuther Library)

rumrunning endeavors.[346] Perhaps one of the most frequently used mobilized ploys by smugglers was that of the milk delivery service. While some were caught in the process of filling milk canisters to the brim with moonshine, others like Newport native Harold Frey were never arrested. As a part of an oral history project conducted by Monroe County Community College in the 1980s, Frey admitted that of the 76, ten-gallon canisters he regularly delivered to a Detroit Creamery "sometimes five or six of those milk cans would be full of whiskey." He recounted he was only stopped once on his milk delivery route by "federals."[347] They took the canvas off the bed of the truck that was covering the iced canisters and checked just the milk cans within reach. Frey and his coworkers knew it was unlikely that the agents would engage in full search and placed the liquor-filled canisters in the middle. Frey also admitted to trucks hauling cases of whiskey between hay bales and area smugglers using telephone trucks to disguise their illegal activities. Not all rumrunners were as successful as Frey. A Detroit driver was arrested in the summer of 1925 when two of his truckloads of coal were found to be covering a significant amount of beer.[348] Even motorized hearse drivers were caught a couple times attempting to transport alcohol under the guise of transporting a corpse.[349]

By 1928, as indicated by the *New York Times*, Windsor area passenger ferries lugged almost twenty million passengers and one million automobiles annually across the Detroit River.[350] Not surprisingly, bootleggers tried to convey their booze to the other side using this popular mode of travel. A couple of Windsor men using the Walkerville Ferry in 1924 were found to be smuggling three cases of beer, five pints of whiskey, three quarts of gin, and one case of port wine in their automobile.[351] Another pair of men with 48 bottles of beer in their car were arrested a year later after they attempted to flee customs officers stationed at the ferry dock.[352] For Detroiter S.S. Kresge, the prominent Anti-Saloon League supporter and millionaire owner of a popular chain of convenience stores, an incident that occurred on November 23, 1927 at the Windsor ferry ramp caused particular embarrassment.[353] Unsettled too was Robert Stranahan, a Toledo native and president of Champion Spark Plug Company. Their sons, both University of Michigan students, were descending the ferry ramp at the foot of Woodward Avenue in Kresge's "luxurious roadster" when they were caught with eleven bottles of liquor. The youthful sybarites were fined a measly $55, but Kresge's beloved car was confiscated and their family names plastered all over the local papers.[354]

The opening of the Ambassador Bridge in November 1929 diverted some of the traffic away from the Detroit River passenger ferries. Thousands of automobiles began to crisscross the international border daily and customs officials routinely searched vehicles for illegal contraband. Soon enough, motorized bootleggers were caught transporting booze across the new route connecting the Motor City with the Border Cities. One of the first rumrunners to be caught on the bridge was a Windsor rumrunner by the name of Albert Gagnon. Eyewitnesses reported that Gagnon almost escaped detection, but a bulging suit jacket pocket aroused suspicion. Dry agents immediately searched Gagnon's vehicle, revealing "bottles hidden in every corner of the automobile." The local bootlegger was fined $250 a few months later.[355] Police blotter reports indicate that officers stationed on the Ambassador Bridge regularly caught drivers smuggling booze.[356]

Just a few months after the opening of the Ambassador Bridge, local newspapers declared the structure to be a tremendous boon for transnational travel and business. On one unseasonably warm February 1930 day, officials counted approximately 18,000 motor vehicles crossing the international border.[357] A few months later, over the July 4th weekend, 2,000 automobiles per hour traversed the Ambassador Bridge.[358] The *Detroit Free Press* lauded the effects of the bridge, asserting "New plants have been established almost daily…This tendency is expected to develop even more rapidly with rapid transporation between the business districts of Windsor and Detroit becoming a reality and a commonplace."[359] Nonetheless, prohibition enforcement was apparently hindering not only the freedom of motorists but also the economic potential of the new international crossing. At a local banquet, the

Cars stream across the Ambassador Bridge, ca 1930. (Photo courtesy the *Detroit News*)

president of the Border Cities Real Estate board shared his displeasure with the "irritating and humiliating inspections" customs officers levied against American and Canadian drivers alike. He claimed the inspections would impede the overall revenue generated and "salutatory effect" of the Ambassador Bridge.[360]

Yet, not everyone took the dry agents stationed on the bridge seriously. Almost exactly one year after the Ambassador Bridge opened, a small cohort of former Hamtramck city officials went for a joyride to a friend's summer home in Windsor. The group thought it would be humorous to put a ketchup bottle in one of the men's front shirt pockets for the return trip home. As expected, they were pulled over on the bridge and a vigorous search ensued. One of the men forgot he had a small bottle of whiskey with a few sips still left in his possession and was subsequently forced to pay an immediate $5 fine. Upon driving away, the men decided to throw the ketchup bottle against a wall for additional hilarity. The customs officials did not find this behavior funny and the Hamtramck group was detained for several hours. Upon their release, one of the joyriding men involved in the "Battle of the Catsup Bottle" was interviewed by the *Detroit Free Press*. He simply stated, "I was not drunk and was not trying to bring in any whiskey to Detroit. There is plenty of whiskey in Detroit without having to go to foreign countries for it."[361]

Despite well-publicized confrontations with drunkards and rumrunners camouflaging themselves with the surrounding automobile culture, it was evident area smugglers continued to possess an advantage over dry agents working the TDW corridor.[362] Rumrunners' ready access to motor vehicles accelerated this advantage. State investigators working in Monroe County admitted booze could be bought anywhere in the vicinity, and it was well known in Toledo that automobilized bootleggers openly plied their trade with little concern.[363] In its July 30, 1928 editorial the *Detroit Free Press* noted that while prohibition enforcement forces increased fivefold along the Detroit River since the beginning of the Volstead era "the liquor supply...seems to be holding out satisfactorily to everyone concerned." The newspaper conceded the rumrunning trade was "expanding even faster than the forces which the government is able to put in the field."[364] Regardless of law enforcement advances during the years of national prohibition, the region's steadfast connection to the automobile industry all but ensured that TDW rumrunners had the expertise and distinctive experiences with motorcars that gave them the upper hand.

The inherent nature of automobility enabled local bootleggers to decide when, where, and how they smuggled illegal alcohol. Dry agents, in turn, could only speculate which roads to patrol, what time rumrunners operated, and the type of vehicles and drivers that were indeed transporting booze. Considering these realities, it was no wonder that the illegal alcohol trade oriented around Detroit employed close to 50,000 local residents and netted $215 million in sales, second only to the automobile industry. Throughout the 1920s, motorcars bolstered the efforts of rumrunners and severely complicated dry enforcement in the region. Ultimately, prohibition's days were numbered on the TDW corridor.[365] The automobility of criminal bootleggers would play a significant role in delivering a deathblow to dry enforcement on the TDW corridor in its final years.[366]

[319] "Deny Getting Ford Police Aid," *Detroit Free Press*, June 12, 1923; "Enforcement Officer's Frown On Navy's Use," *Detroit Free Press*, June 12, 1923

[320] "Tell Dry Men to Use Guns," *Toledo News-Bee*, June 6, 1923; "Claim Pointing of Firearms," *Toledo News-Bee*, December 29, 1923.

[321]"Seize Rum in Ecorse Sans Warrant - Hurd," *Detroit Free Press*, July 27, 1923.

[322] "Hundred Gallons of Liquor Found in Automobile," *Monroe Evening News*, July 1924; "Rum Laden Car; No Warrant, No Case," *Detroit Free Press*, June 15, 1923; "Liquor Arrest Pact is Denied," *Detroit Free Press*, April 18, 1922; "Lack of Search Warrant by Cop Frees Hooch Man," *Detroit Free Press*, August 21, 1923.

[323] "Truck Driver is Discharged by Court," *Monroe Evening News*, July 29, 1924.

[324] "Highest Court Upholds Rum Auto Search," *Detroit Free Press*, March 3, 1925.

[325] "Search Ruled O.K., Rum War Pushed," *Detroit Free Press*, March 4, 1925.

[326] "The People of the State of Michigan vs. Howard Edwards," November 10, 1927, Circuit Court Archives, Monroe County Courthouse.

[327] "The People of the State of Michigan vs. Alex Horowitz," December 27, 1927, Circuit Court Archives, Monroe County Courthouse.

[328] "The People of the State of Michigan vs. Ed Nadeau," November 4, 1927, Circuit Court Archives, Monroe County Courthouse.

[329] "The People of the State of Michigan vs. Harold McNamara," April 10, 1928, Circuit Court Archives, Monroe County Courthouse.

[330] "Search Ruled O.K., Rum War Pushed," *Detroit Free Press*, March 4, 1925.

[331] "Rum Runner Tells of Booze Flow Through Canadian Line Huts," *Salt Lake Telegram*, May 26, 1923; "Michigan State Police Outlaws on Land and Sea," *Detroit Free Press*, August 16, 1925; "Dry Patrols Here in Chaos, Baxter Says," *Detroit Free Press*, April 6 1927; "Our Rum Capital: An Amazing Picture," *New York Times*, May 27, 1928.

[332] J. Anne Funderburg, *Bootleggers and Beer Barons of the Prohibition,* (Jefferson, North Carolina: McFarland, 2014), 41-48.

[333] "U.S. Sleuths with Speed Boat, Auto, to Hunt Booze Runners," *Sandusky Star-Journal*, July 22, 1920; "Will Purchase Automobile for Use of Police," *Monroe Evening News*, March 10, 1925; " 'Tin Cans' are Used in the Case of Bandits," *Toledo News-Bee*, January 25, 1921; "New Automobile is Bought for Use of Police," *Monroe Evening News*, March 14, 1925.

[334] "11 Stills, 6 Men Taken in Raid," *Toledo News-Bee*, June 11, 1927; "Police in Chase Nab Two as Rum Runners," *Toledo News-Bee*, June 20, 1927; "Two Ohio Men Held for Transporting Rum," *Detroit Free Press*, December 23, 1925; "Customs Agents Seize Beer Trucks," *Detroit Free Press*, October 28, 1928; "106 Murderers Held in Year," *Detroit Free Press*, January 1, 1925; "Prohibition Enforcement in Detroit," *Detroit Free Press*, July 30, 1928; "Flappers Run Border Rum, Officers Say," *Detroit Free Press*, February 19, 1928.

[335] "Profits Scant, Grief Plentiful, Booze Vendors Say," *Detroit Free Press*, August 16, 1925.

[336] "Rum Car Sale Stings Buyer; He Likes Odor," *Detroit Free Press*, May 29, 1920; "Simons Orders Sale of Seized Rum Cars," *Detroit Free Press*, December 9, 1926.

[337] "Liquor Theft May End Kirk Auto Towing," *Toledo News-Bee*, June 28, 1927; "Auto Bargain Hunters," *Detroit Free Press*, August 27, 1929.

[338] "Sues for Booze Car," *Sandusky Register*, January 5, 1930; "Police Probe Federal Sale of Rum Cars," *Detroit Free Press*, April 30, 1930; "Federals Laugh at Police Probe," *Detroit Free Press*, May 1, 1930.

[339] "Ontario Now Opens the Beer Spigot," *New York Times*, May 17, 1925.

[340] "Detroit Man is Freed in Rum-Toting Charge," *Detroit Free Press*, April 13, 1923; "US Jails 4 in Rum Raids," *Detroit Free Press*, November 7, 1924; "Police Seize Big 'Canadian Beer' Plant," *Detroit Free Press*, October 1, 1924; "Smuggler Cut Prices, Jailed," *Detroit Free Press*, September 28, 1924.

[341] "Gassing Rum Car Seized in Michigan," *New York Times*, April 29, 1928; "Rum Runners' Poison Gas Car Captured," *Detroit Free Press*, April 29, 1928.

[342] "Booze Runners Plan Heavy Traffic Here This Winter," *Detroit Free Press*, September 21, 1924; "Two Detroiters Held on Liquor Charges," *Detroit Free Press*, June 17, 1928.

[343] "Flappers Run Border Rum, Officers Say," *Detroit Free Press*, February 19, 1928; "Girl Bootleggers Present New Social Problem," *Detroit Free Press*, December 2, 1923; "Girl, 20, Liquor Car Pilot, Held," *Detroit Free Press*, February 19, 1926.

[344] "Girl Rum Runner Uses Pistol Here," *Monroe Evening News*, January 29, 1926.

[345] "Rum Pilot Machine Hits Officers' Car, Toledo Woman Hurt," March 29, 1927; "Women Sentenced as Rum Violators by Circuit Judge," *Monroe Evening News*, November 5, 1927; "2 Girls Captured in Rum Car Chase," *Detroit Free Press*, December 31, 1927; "Rum Queen, 8 Others Held in Gang Cleanup," *Toledo News-Bee*, June 2, 1928; "Man, Grandmother Held in Rum Car," *Detroit Free Press*, September 2, 1928; "Monroe Youths and Liquor Nabbed on Way to Columbus," *Detroit Free Press*, January 9, 1926; "Girl and Boy Nabbed in Rum Cars are Held," *Detroit Free Press*, March 5, 1929.

[346] "Still is Seized as Plot Clue," *Detroit Free Press*, July 23, 1928.

[347] Harold Frey to Sally Gedelian, *Monroe County Oral History Project*, March 2, 1986.

[348] Ibid.

[349] "U.S. Holds Alleged Beer Truck Driver," *Detroit Free Press*, July 24, 1925; "Liquor Laden Motor Hearse Taken in Raid," *Detroit Free Press*, June 12, 1926; "Halt Hearse, Mourners Flee, 'Corpse' is Beer," *Detroit Free Press*, August 17, 1926.

[350] "Our 'Rum Capital': An Amazing Picture," *New York Times*, May 27, 1928.

[351] "Customs Officers Halt Rum Auto," *Detroit Free Press*, January 17, 1924.

[352] "Customs 'Cop' Gets Joy Ride Ride in Booze Car," *Detroit Free Press*, March 27, 1925.

[353] "Seize Rum on 3 in Car on Kresge License," *Detroit Free Press*, November 24, 1927; "Youth Gives Kresge Name," *Border Cities Star*, November 24, 1927.

[354] "Toledo Youth Hits Rum Snag," *Toledo News-Bee*, November 25, 1927.

[355] "Gagnon Comes Up January 20," *The Windsor Star*, Jan 13, 1930; "15 Fined $7,500 in Rum Cases," *Detroit Free Press*, April 20, 1930.

[356] "95 Quarts, Pints Seized on Bridge," *Detroit Free Press*, January 12, 1930; "Two in Armed Car Undergoing Check," *Detroit Free Press*, February 28, 1930; "Car, 25 Cases, Seized Upon Bridge," *Detroit Free Press*, May 15, 1930; "Find Rum Concealed in Windsor's Man Car," *Detroit Free Press*, July 24, 1930.

[357] "Traffic Rush Starts Early," *Detroit Free Press*, February 24, 1930.

[358] "Traffic Sets New Record," *Detroit Free Press*, July 5, 1930.

[359] "Immense Influence of New Bridge Cited," *Detroit Free Press*, January 12, 1930.

[360] "Protest is Voiced Over Bridge Rules," *Detroit Free Press*, January 26, 1930.

[361] "Catsup Bottle Case is Ended in Silence," *Detroit Free Press*, November 15, 1930.

[362] "Hearing Bears Vices in Monroe," *Detroit Free Press*, September 23, 1927.

[363] "Jennings' 'Cleanup' Is Seen As Comeback for Move to 'Get' Him," *Toledo News-Bee*, November 18, 1927.

[364] "Prohibition Enforcement in Detroit," *Detroit Free Press*, July 30, 1928.

[365] Philip P. Mason, *RumRunning and the Roaring Twenties: Prohibition on the Michigan-Ontario Waterway* (Detroit: Wayne State University Press, 1995) 145.

[366] Daniel Okrent, *Last Call: The Rise and Fall of Prohibition*, (New York: Scribner, 2010), 256-257.

CHAPTER 15
Crime Wave: Hijackings and Murder in the Volstead Era

Sometime during the night of April 3, 1927, a man was forced out of an automobile on an isolated Monroe County road just north of the Michigan-Ohio line and shot six times. Local newspapers chalked it up as yet "another killing" in a growing "bootleg war" that was spreading throughout the TDW corridor. The deceased man, sharply dressed in a navy pinstripe suit and sporting a grey cap, could not be immediately identified despite business cards and letters found in his pockets.[367]

The next day it was revealed that the local man was Charles Ebner, a widower, father of three, and a used automobile dealer in Point Place. The man's vehicle was found abandoned in Toledo with several cases of empty beer bottles in the trunk. Police questioned his three boys—all under the age of eight—who revealed a haunting story. According to Ebner's oldest sons, mysterious men had been coming and going with their dad in different automobiles throughout the day Sunday. On Monday morning, the mysterious men "roused them out of bed and made them build a fire." Next, they ordered the oldest boy, Charles Jr., to retrieve a newspaper from the Casino across the street. Upon the boy's return, the "tall man read them a story about their father being killed," despite the fact their father's body was not found until after the printing of Monday's morning paper. The Toledo police vaguely stated that those who took Charles Ebner on his "death ride" likely had a "secret jealous motive."[368]

Abandoned bodies continued to be found on regional roadsides and isolated locations for the remainder of the Volstead era.[369] These corpses became stark symbols of the shocking violence that gripped the area, provoking many local residents to discern not only whether prohibition was enforceable but also whether dry enforcement was the cause of widespread lawlessness. Several historians of the prohibition era have indeed already argued that the public's abhorrence of overt violence and corruption was a driving impetus behind the repeal movement.[370] Nonetheless, these same historians have largely overlooked the central role that motorcars played in the rise of gangland crime and booze-related bribery. The most violent episodes and troubling instances of police profiteering were usually rooted in the area's automobility. Close analysis of dry enforcement events and developments on the TDW corridor reveal just how regional prohibition was "taken for a drive," ending the area's dry days for good.[371]

Starting in 1927, many across the country and along the corridor started to discuss the so-called "crime wave" and engaged in debates about whether federal prohibition was its root cause. In a speech to lawyers in Toledo, William Gibbs McAdoo—a prominent American statesman, leading attorney, and the son-in-law of former U.S. president Woodrow Wilson—declared "machine politicians" fueled the surge in violent and corrupt behavior, not dry laws.[372] In his 1927 speech to the Detroit City College, Police Commissioner William Rutledge downplayed the rise in booze-related crime by redirecting his audience to consider what was happening on local streets. To support his point, the Commissioner shared how the 325 murders within the city's limits were actually eclipsed by the 392 traffic deaths in Detroit the previous year. "Our biggest crime wave is the slaughter of innocents by automobiles," Rutledge stressed.[373]

Conversely, some dry and wet advocates pointed to the ineffectiveness of prohibition enforcement as the driving impetus for the crime wave. One Detroit native's letter to the editor of the *Detroit Free Press* stumped for stricter enforcement, claiming that it was "the 'raging' effect" of bootleg intoxicants that prompted the continuous "pulling of the trigger." A member of the Michigan state prison commission also pointed to the lack of meaningful dry enforcement "as the legitimate parent of and the direct and indirect cause of the greatest crime wave ever known."[374] The state official went a step further, however, declaring that the federal prohibition "law itself encourages, invites, and breeds crime" and that it needed modification or repeal.[375]

Regardless of what actually prompted this crime wave, momentous events happening in the Canadian Border Cities area only contributed to the surge in overt criminal behavior on the TDW corridor. Ontario's provincial government repealed many of its Prohibition regulations, enabling government-owned stores to sell intoxicating beverages to the public. Thousands of thirsty American and Canadian motorists flooded Windsor in the first weeks of June to visit its two licensed liquor stores. While visitors to these depots left with smiles, professional rumrunners and blind pig operators watched with anger. Besides being promoted as a deliberate campaign to "put the bootlegger out of business," Ontario's Liquor Control Act (LCA) hurt those involved in the TDW illegal alcohol trade in several ways. First, many of their American customers could now directly purchase their own booze without having to visit a speakeasy or deal with a gun-toting smuggler.[376] Secondly, Ontario's beer and liquor prices were reasonably low, forcing rumrunners and blind pig operators to reduce their own prices. "Beer parlor men" admitted to the *Border Cities Star* that prior to the passage of the LCA they could sell a bottle of beer for 50 cents. Now with "government control competition," they had to mark down beer prices to 33 cents a bottle. In turn, the profit margins for professional bootleggers and the locations they supplied were reduced as well.[377]

Perhaps most importantly, Windsor area enforcement officials were being pushed to crack down on rumrunners and illegal alcohol sales. Since the early 1920s and the Spracklin fiasco, the Border Cities region was essentially a worry-free zone for professional smugglers and speakeasy owners. Due to a lack of prohibition policing on Canadian soil, Detroit bootleggers operated on the saying "If you are going to Windsor, leave your guns on this side."[378] However, after the implementation of the LCA, provincial officials and a local newspaper began to pressure those responsible for enforcing the new dry laws. Mark Hannah, chairman of the Ontario Liquor Commission, stated that he was committed to "putting the bootlegger out of business" during a summer visit to Windsor.[379]

After a few months of lackluster prohibition enforcement, the *Border Cities Star* decided on September 8, 1927 to publish an editorial entitled "All Citizens, Attention!" The area's largest newspaper was calling out both the Windsor and Provincial police, declaring that their pledges to stop booze-related crime "nothing but a hollow sham." The *Border Cities Star* pleaded with those charged with enforcing the new LCA, writing it was the newspaper's "sincere hope that the authorities will move, before things have gone too far, to prevent our riverfront—and some inland thoroughfares as well—from becoming avenues of blatant illegality."[380]

Just a few days later, a special hearing was called by General Victor Williams of the Ontario Provincial Police. Though Williams admitted the region was "under policed," he also argued the newspaper's "charges have cast a great slur on the administration of the law in the Border Cities."[381] In the same meeting, Windsor's Police Magistrate, William Gundy, countered the newspaper's claims. "*The Star* grossly exaggerate[s] the situation in Windsor and that the conditions which do exist are being met by the fullest measure of law enforcement which the officers can bring to bear," Gundy averred.[382]

The next day Howard Ferguson, Ontario's Premier, struck a decidedly different tone. He announced at a local picnic that he was fully committed to driving out all regional bootleggers and that he would devote "all the force and all the treasure the government has" if needed.[383] Sure enough, the increased pressure on the provincial and city police prompted a surge in enforcement. From September 8 to October 8, hundreds of blind pig operators and others involved in the illegal liquor trade were arrested, jailed, and fined. Roadhouses known as bootlegger and gambling dens also closed up in rapid succession.[384]

Though the wave of vigorous policing ultimately died down, Border Cities' officers would continue to enforce the dry laws at a much more regular rate until 1933. This simple change in enforcement practices transformed the nature of the bootlegging business on the TDW corridor. No longer could smugglers operate as freely on Canadian soil as they used to in years past. Rumrunning routes began to close up at their source, causing gangs of criminal smugglers to aggressively compete over contested territory and a smaller number of American customers who did not want to make quick jaunt over the border to purchase alcohol. Not surprisingly, the *Border Cities Star* reported that "rival interests in the trans-river rush" were plotting against each other at the end of 1927. Hijackings, shootings, corruption, and brutal killings ensued for the last six years of prohibition on the TDW corridor. Shrouded by the shocking headlines and uptick in community concern was the fact that regional automobility played an important role in the surge of criminality.[385]

A noticeable increase in violent hijackings throughout the TDW corridor revealed the connection between prohibition-era criminality and motorcar culture. By stealing stocks of liquor and fleeing the scene in automobiles, desperate rumrunners could undersell their competitors, as illustrated early in 1926 by a trio of gangsters who terrorized small-time bootleggers in Grosse Pointe, Michigan.[386] Some tasked with transporting booze were lucky enough to survive encounters with hijackers. In 1928, while steering a load of $6,700 of liquor from Windsor, George Minall and John Corvell were followed by a large touring car. As the vehicles arrived at a "lonely section" of the highway, the trailing car pulled up alongside and the gangsters inside brandished revolvers. The rumrunner wisely pulled over and gave up the truck without a fight.[387] A pair of bootlegging Detroit brothers were lucky enough to survive two booze-related kidnappings in a matter of a month. On the second occasion, while they were leading a smuggling caravan of motor trucks outside Detroit's city limits, a gang armed with sawed-off shotguns ambushed them. The brothers lost four truckloads of whiskey valued at $25,000.[388]

Even those who were not actively engaged in the transportation of booze sometimes became victims of local hijacking incidents. Fully automobilized holdup men, "masquerad[ing] as police officers," swooped down upon Detroit area speakeasy operators and seized their illegal stocks at gunpoint.[389] Across the river in Amherstburg, an eighteen-year-old male was severely beaten by eleven men angered over the loss of their liquor. Apparently their cache of booze, stored in the vicinity of the teen's homestead, had been taken away by hijackers in a truck. The gangsters madly searched the premises for two hours before turning to the teen with questions he could not answer. Speeding away in three cars bearing Michigan licenses, the men left the boy with a broken nose, two fractured ribs, and bruises all over his body.[390]

Not everyone was as lucky as the Amherstburg youth. After a violent holdup of a Detroit "soft drink parlor" left two bartenders dead, several days later the body of Joseph Yeomans, a known hijacker, was found floating in a lagoon off of Belle Isle. Yeomans had been mortally wounded in the holdup earlier that week. His accomplices dragged him out of the speakeasy, entered a waiting motorcar, and drove Yeomans' lifeless body to a secluded area of Belle Isle.[391] The *Detroit Free Press* reported Yeomans had recently changed his criminal occupation from rumrunning to hijacking, reflecting the difficulty of making profits as a traditional bootlegger.[392]

A few years later, in 1932, a gruesome death was reported by newspapers in Toledo. The body of Jimmy Lahey, a local liquor smuggler, was found just north of the state line with four bullets "pumped" into his head and a fifth "lodged into his neck."[393] In the week before his murder, "reliable information" indicated Lahey hijacked a booze car traveling between Cleveland and Detroit. On the day of his disappearance, witnesses claim Lahey was herded into an expensive sedan in downtown Toledo. With five empty shells found at the crime scene, it was clear to law enforcement the "well known police character" had been "taken for a ride."[394]

Violent hijackings aroused concern in those charged with enforcing dry laws. Before his own murder, Lahey had survived two attempts on his life in 1931. In both instances, armed gangsters in automobiles pulled up alongside Lahey's vehicle and sprayed it with gunfire. On the second occasion his friend—who reportedly "had no connection whatever with the underworld"—was shot and killed.[395] Afterwards, the *Toledo News-Bee* made note of how the "bungling guns of gangland" spurred every police agency in the Glass City on a mission "to rid Toledo of the menace or rule of mob and murder."[396]

The 1927 murder of a young man during a booze hijacking in Detroit caused quite an uproar. "The ruthless killing of the youth brought out a storm of protest yesterday from all sources," reported the *Detroit Free Press*.[397] Following Lahey's well-publicized murder, Toledo's police chief Louis Haas announced an aggressive campaign to end the egregious endeavors of the area's automobilized criminals. "Every man on the department has orders to pick up known hoodlums and I want the police officers to carry out these orders to the letter," declared Haas.[398]

---

[367] "Body Found Drilled by Six Bullets," *Toledo News-Bee*, April 4, 1927.

[368] "Jealousy Seen as Motive Behind Brutal Murder of Point Place Dealer," *Toledo News-Bee*, April 5, 1927.

[369] Philip Mason, *Rum-Running and the Roaring Twenties: Prohibition on the Michigan-Ontario Waterway*, (Detroit: Wayne State University, 1995), 146.

[370] Lisa McGirr, *The War on Alcohol: Prohibition and the Rise of the American State*, (New York: W.W. Norton, 2016), 162-163, 187-193.

[371] Daniel Okrent, *Last Call: The Rise and Fall of Prohibition*, (New York: Scribner, 2010), 320-321; *Temperance or Prohibtion?*, (New York City: The Hearst Temperance Contest Committee, 1929) 170-187.

[372] "McAdoo Says Attack on Dry Law Camoflauge of Machine Politics to Boss Country," *Detroit Free Press*, January 18, 1927.

[373] "Detroit Auto Toll Continues to Gain," *Border Cities Star*, April 28, 1927.

[374] "Trace Crime Wave to Supply of Whisky," *Detroit Free Press*, February 11, 1927.

[375] "Says Dry Law Breeds Crime," *Detroit Free Press*, January 17, 1930.

[376] "Excuse Days Are Over," *The Border Cities Star,* June 14, 1927.

[377] "Prices of Beer in Blindpigs Slump," *The Border Cities Star*, July 22, 1927.

[378] "Magistrate Gundy's Report in Full," *Border Cities Star*, September 14, 1927.

[379] "Liquor Head Visits City," *Border Cities Star*, June 11, 1927.

[380] "All Citizens, Attention!," *Border Cities Star*, September 8, 1927.

[381] "Declared the Star Blocked Raids on Gamblers," *Border Cities Star*, September 14, 1927.

[382] "Magistrate Gundy's Report in Full," *Border Cities Star*, September 14, 1927.

[383] "Premier to 'Clean' Up Border," *Border Cities Star*, September 15, 1927.

[384] "An Astounding Story Printed in the Public Interest," *Border Cities Star*, October 8, 1927.

[385] "Rum Feud Scouted by Customs Men," *Border Cities Star*, December 14, 1927.

[386] "Holdups Laid to 3 Arrested as Hijackers," *Detroit Free Press,* January 23, 1926.

[387] "Hijackers Nab Liquor Truck," *Border Cities Star*, May 13, 1928.

[388] "Nine Arrested for Kidnapping," *Detroit Free Press*, October 13, 1927.

[389] "Ten Hijacking Suspects Held," *Detroit Free Press*, January 10, 1933.

[390] "Liquor Gang Attacks Youth," *Detroit Free Press*, December 12, 1930.

[391] "Weekend Shootings Cause Three Deaths," *Detroit Free Press,* December 2, 1929.

[392] "Identify Body Found on Isle," *Detroit Free Press*, December 8, 1929.

[393] "Jimmy Lahey Slain by Gang Near Toledo," *Toledo News-Bee*, March 16, 1932.

[394] "Drive on Gangs Starts After Youth is Slain," *Toledo News-Bee*, May 11, 1931.

[395] "Blame Liquor Feud in Killing," *Detroit Free Press*, December 10, 1927.

[396] "Jimmy Lahey Slain by Gang Near Toledo," *Toledo News-Bee*, March 16, 1932.

[397] "Blame Liquor Feud in Killing," *Detroit Free Press*, December 10, 1927.

[398] Ibid.

CHAPTER 16
Easier Said Than Done: Policing in the Late Prohibition Years on the TDW Corridor

Aggressive policing on the TDW corridor was easier said than done. Due to the nature of automobilized hijacking cases, local officers were increasingly compelled to extend their communications beyond their jurisdiction to other law enforcement agencies throughout the region. In early 1928, the shooting of two Detroit brothers, who led an "extensive hijacking and blackmailing organization," put officers on both sides of the Detroit River on high alert. The Detroit Police immediately notified Canadian authorities of the crime, spurring the "full strength" of police in Sandwich to guard the house of a prominent Border Cities liquor exporter, who the assassins allegedly planned to "take for a ride."[399]

The 1929 arrest of a quartet of Toledo booze hijackers in Monroe also demonstrated the need for improved communication between TDW enforcement agencies. The four gangsters were first spotted by local police entering a Trenton "beer spot" with revolvers in their hands. Surprised by the presence of Trenton cops, they quickly ran from the scene and sped away in a "powerful gray touring car" that was parked at the curbside. After a three block "fugitive car" chase, the Trenton officers opted to call ahead to the Michigan State Police stationed in Rockwood. By the time they were able to place the call to the troopers, the speeding motorcar had already roared through the small village. The Rockwood police, in turn, phoned ahead to the Monroe police. When the Toledo gangsters reached that city, law enforcement finally halted their vehicle. The men surrendered without a fight after the 20-mile jaunt. Dry agents were "convinced" that the quartet was responsible for numerous liquor hijackings in the Downriver area.[400]

Policing during prohibition became even more challenging with the annual onslaught of winter and the usual freezing over of local waterways. Rather than just patrolling regional roads, automobilized dry enforcers were perplexed with how they could halt the rum-running traffic buzzing back and forth from Canada on the ice. One longtime Monroe County resident noted how, as a young girl, she would watch from her lakefront cottage the dozens of booze-toting cars that descended upon the frozen shore "like a flock of blackbirds."[401]

Officers outside of the South Rockwood detachment of the Michigan State Police. (Photo courtesy Rockwood Area Historical Museum)

Officers must have been worried about their safety on the frozen lake because their smuggling counterparts took extra precautions to prevent their own drowning. Harold Stotz, an area farmer, made note of one mechanic who modified vehicles for traveling across the ice. Rumrunners would purchase an "old Model T ... which they could buy for very little," and the mechanic would strip it of any unnecessary weight and cut off the doors.[402]

For smugglers, the trek over to Canada was somewhat dangerous, but it was the return home that was especially harrowing. Once the crates of booze were loaded into the hollowed out motorcar, the weight of the vehicle sometimes doubled or tripled. These daring drivers had to be especially vigilant for "bad spot[s] on the ice" and had to be ready to jump out of their doorless car if they felt a sudden descent downward. One Border Cities bootlegger attested to some of these rumrunners also hauling long wooden planks on each side of the car, which could be used to cross gaping chasms in the ice.[403]

One *Detroit News* journalist in February of 1930 watched on with interest as "nearly 75 automobiles, "most of them beer- and liquor-laden" made the crossing from Amherstburg to various points along the Detroit River and Lake Erie shoreline in a matter of two hours. "Not all were bound for Michigan," the reporter noted. "About a tenth bore Ohio license plates and their course was down river, to Toledo and points east." The journalist was able to interview one of the brave smugglers making the icy crossing. He admitted, "the law isn't the thing we fear most. What we are really afraid of is the ice. Any time it may give way beneath and let one of us through." The *Detroit News* also made note that instead of enforcing prohibition, some agents opted to go across and obtain their own alcohol.[404]

Local law enforcement routinely placed their life in danger during the final years of prohibition. On June 28, 1928, a River Rouge constable was shot in the jaw when he deliberately stepped into the crossfire of a prominent rumrunner and a known hijacker. Both criminals were killed in the gunfight. A year later, a patrolman walking his beat in downtown Detroit halted a "liquor car" that ignored a red light. Apparently, the officer was not aware that the vehicle was part of a larger bootlegging convoy. While speaking with the driver of the stopped vehicle, another automobilized smuggler plowed into the officer. Luckily, the patrolman survived the incident with just a "possible fractured skull." Other law enforcement agents working on the TDW corridor were not as lucky.

Near the port of Toledo later that year, a U.S. Marshal was shot and killed by rumrunners while attempting to stop the transfer of booze from a boat to a truck waiting on shore. In 1928, gunmen abducted, shot, and dumped the body of a Detroit officer at a Hamtramck intersection. The assassins reportedly were hired by local blind pig operators. Just north

An editorial cartoon by Percy Cromwell lampooning the efforts of law enforcement in their battles with bootleggers. (Image courtesy University of Michigan, Bentley Historical Library)

of the Motor City, Grosse Pointe Policemen Erdhardt Myer and Claude Lanstrsa fell victim on June 1, 1930 to a "fusillade" of bullets when they attempted to pull over a group of gangsters who had just hit an elderly woman with their "expensive coupe." For one of the resulting funeral services, the presiding Catholic priest lamented the plight of Prohibition era cops. "Compared with the men our police officers of today must face day and night, Jesse James and his gang were seraphs confirmed in grace," proclaimed Fr. Vincent O'Toole. "I charge that prohibition is responsible for all this, because prohibition has made organized murder a lucrative profession."[405]

Increasingly, a sizeable proportion of dry agents and local officers working on the TDW corridor opted to enforce prohibition half-heartedly or not at all. Many experienced firsthand the folly of exerting themselves or even witnessed partners dying for a law they realized could not be enforced in the age of the automobile. Customs patrolman Howard Baker learned this lesson the hard way. "Known as one of the best officers in the customs patrol and feared by rumrunners everywhere," Baker took his job on the Detroit riverfront quite seriously. On one fateful night in 1929, Baker was engaged in an automobile chase with a speeding rumrunner when his patrol vehicle was forced off the road. Baker suffered severe injuries, leaving him crippled and paralyzed on one side of his face. Compensation payments were not nearly enough and he was ultimately let go from his post. A year later Baker, ten dry agents, and five other downriver rumrunners were charged with orchestrating a vast "conspiracy to violate the dry laws" in southeast Michigan and beyond. [406]

Corruption, graft, and bribery on the TDW corridor plagued dry enforcement and eroded public confidence in the efficacy of prohibition as a whole. Close analysis of regional police corruption cases reveals how automobility placed officers in the position to make considerable illegal profits if they were willing. A special hearing to remove Monroe

County's sheriff and other local government officials from office in 1927 and 1928 illustrated the connection between prohibition era graft and motorcar culture. The case against Monroe County law enforcement and others began with the unsettling discovery of the body of local man. An undercover investigation was conducted and it revealed extensive booze related criminal operations that involved some level of complicity from local enforcement. The special grand jury presiding over the case charged Sheriff Joseph Kinsey, some of his deputies, and former prosecuting attorney William Haas with "extort[ing] money from persons engaged in the transportation and possession of liquors...and releasing them and their vehicles upon payment of cash."[407]

As the public trial commenced, testimonies unveiled widespread and wanton disregard for dry laws in the area, prompting the *Detroit Free Press* to call Monroe a "modern Gomorrah." More specifically, testimonies from known rumrunners detailed allegedly how corrupt authorities utilized the automoibilized aspect of bootlegging to their financial advantage. Roland Wilson, a local rumrunner, testified that one winter he and another smuggler were arrested transporting booze across frozen Lake Erie. Upon conferring with his lawyer, William Haas, Wilson

A truck smuggling booze from Canada partially fell through the ice, spilling its contents. (Photo courtesy Wayne State University, Walter P. Reuther Library)

was asked to fork over $200. When Wilson questioned the payment, Haas reportedly ordered him to "kccp [his] mouth shut."[408] Wilson and his partner were released the next day without formal charges or a court appearance. It was understood the money was divided between Haas, Sheriff Kinsey, and the arresting deputies.[409]

On another occasion, Monroe county native Hank Fountain abandoned his liquor-laden automobile as two deputies approached his position. His vehicle was confiscated, but a letter received from Haas two days later indicated that Fountain could recover his beloved motorcar for just $200. Fountain paid up and retrieved his auto from a local car sales agency. Jack Perry, a Toledo rumrunner, was arrested with 90 gallons of moonshine in his vehicle. A payment of $200 garnered his release the next day and his car was given back. Other local smugglers attested to the fact that they evaded arrest in their vehicles because their liquor bosses had paid off area enforcement.[410]

Ultimately, Michigan Governor Fred Green exonerated Sheriff Kinsey and everyone else named in the conspiracy charges. In his official statement, Green declared:

> While it appears that Sheriff Kinsey has not been as vigorous as he might have been in the enforcement of the laws, that he was lax in the administration and discipline of his office, that the actions of some of his subordinantes have on a number of instances been of such a character as to merit adverse criticism, yet I am not convinced that there has been any wilful or deliberate intent on his part to violate his oath of office or the criminal laws of this state.[411]

In other words, Governor Green thought Kinsey, Haas, and some local officers had fallen short of their prohibition enforcement responsibilities, but there was not sufficient evidence that they purposefully engaged in illegal activities with area rumrunners. The prosecution's only witnesses were rumrunning criminals of "very low order" and there was not any definitive proof their payments to Haas were transferred to local law enforcement.[412]

Dozens of other officers working on the TDW corridor did not escape the corruption charges levied against them.[413] One of the most troubling examples was that of River Rouge resident and Detroit policeman Alozy Dolney. In June 1928, Dolney and three accomplices dressed like Michigan State troopers and stalked a well-traveled highway connecting Detroit and Chicago in their own vehicle. When they spotted a "heavily loaded beer truck," Dolney and his companions pulled over the vehicle at gunpoint. As it was customary, the smugglers offered a bribe of $120, or $1 per case. Dolney instead demanded $500 while his other cronies visibly began to hijack the bootleggers' truck. Having seen enough, one of the rumrunners pulled a pistol from a trouser pocket and shot Dolney in the shoulder. The shooter turned himself in and Dolney's story of deceit was exposed in the courts and the *Detroit Free Press*. After it was revealed his quartet was well known for preying on "hard-working, honest" rumrunners, Dolney was dismissed from the force.[414] Two years later a life of graft also caught up to John Dohr, a U.S. Marshal who worked out of Maumee, near Toledo. After he and some of his deputies confiscated a truckload of expensive champagne and wine from Toledo bootlegger Jackie Kennedy, he turned around and sold the booze to a local businessman. It also was revealed that Dohr and his subordinates were also accepting payments for the release of confiscated liquor vehicles.[415]

In the face of rampant corruption charges and the recent surge in booze-related violence, some devoted dry agents—hoping to validate their work—urged government officials to supply them with resources that reflected the reality of enforcing prohibition in the late 1920s and early 1930s. In 1928, the Toledo police department not only acquired more automobiles and motorcycles to keep up with the automobilized nature of bootlegging, but they also purchased ten bullet proof vests and ten machine guns "capable of firing 935 bullets a minute."

Oscar Olander, Michigan's Commissioner of Public Safety, expressed concern about the vulnerability of his State troopers, especially those working on isolated highways streaming out of the Motor City. "We have been forced to fight the machine guns with revolvers and pursue eight-cylinder automobiles with cars of six cylinders," complained Olander. "The rumrunners use the most modern and fastest equipment possible." Olander's pleas were soon answered. A few months later, his officers were supplied with three armored, high-powered vehicles, each equipped with machine guns, bombs, and other militaristic features.[416]

It is hard to determine if the ramping up of enforcement influenced an uptick of controversial policing as area residents began to complain about overzealous cops. A lengthy 1929 *Detroit Free Press* letter to the editor described legitimate concerns about policing practices on regional roadways. The writer, a Toledo resident, shared how in the course of three weeks his vehicle was pulled over three times by liquor agents in Michigan. All three times the deputies or federal officers were wearing civilian clothes, spurring indecision on his part to pull over. On the final occasion, the deputies were not wearing uniforms nor their badges and

Members of the Toledo Police Department's motorcycle squad, ca 1920. (Photo courtesy the Toledo-Lucas County Public Library, Images in Time)

they also utilized a Studebaker automobile with an Ohio license plate to affect the traffic stop. After revealing these scenarios, the Toledo writer explained his concerns to the *Free Press'* readers. Not only was he worried about being pulled over by armed highwaymen in the future but he also fretted over his indecision to stop his car, possibly prompting aggressive officers to use lethal force. The man concluded that the vast majority of law-abiding motorists "should be allowed to travel over the highways without being molested and without endangering our lives and property."[417]

A year earlier, the community of St. Clair Shores—situated just north of Detroit—filed a formal letter of protest with the U.S. district attorney due to the "intimidating and vexatious actions" of prohibition agents working in their town. Dry officers were accused of punching a newspaper deliveryman in the jaw after an inspection of his vehicle and shooting at another innocent truck driver that hesitated to stop. Agents also engaged in a blatantly illegal search of a local mechanic's garage. In quasi-military style, two automobiles quickly pulled up to the business, unloading several officers who surrounded the garage with guns drawn. Upon the agents' entry into his building, the owner "asked for credentials." Without a search warrant to present, the officers opted to beat the man up. The policing situation had deteriorated so badly that St. Clair Shores motorists began to carry guns with them as they traveled about town. The protest letter declared that the agents' "untoward and menacing conduct have become a source of intimidation, terrorism and constant danger of violence to our citizens lawfully exercising their right to use of the public highway."[418]

Dry officers' use of firearms in regional rumrunning cases during the final years of prohibition also provoked considerable controversy. The February 23, 1929 *Detroit Free Press* headline screamed in bold letters, "Border Guards Held for Shooting of Ecorse Citizen," following the wounding of a motorist in Wyandotte. The two border patrol agents involved were indeed held for questioning and were almost charged with reckless firearms usage. Pursuing a liquor-laden truck in their own patrol automobile, the agents claimed that an Ecorse motorist purposefully blocked their path. The officers decided to shoot their revolvers in the direction of the impeding vehicle. One of the bullets passed through the back window and grazed the driver's face, prompting the Ecorse man to veer off the road. Luckily for the officers, the victim decided not to press charges.[419] A year earlier, off the Lake Erie coast near the Monroe County farming village of Newport, state police opened fire and killed a man steering a vehicle as part of a liquor convoy across the ice. An investigation concluded the officers acted in self-defense. Other reports indicated that agents expended dozens of bullets in some car chases with smugglers on busy roadways. Shootings were apparently so common along the Detroit River that Canadian motorists living in the Border Cities feared for their lives driving along the shore.[420]

Especially troubling to regional law enforcement at the end of the dry era were the substantial number of drunk drivers on the region's roads. From 1927 to 1933, area newspapers contained plentiful reports of intoxicated motorists. The Canadian Border Cities, in particular, dealt with an influx of American drivers beginning in 1927 when they started to cross the international border to engage in legal consumption of booze. Accordingly, foreign intoxicated automobilists began to cause problems on local roadways. For example, on December 14, 1927, a drunk driver from Detroit steered his vehicle onto a set of railroad tracks near Windsor, breaking through numerous signal posts, halting two freight trains, and ultimately smashing into another automobile.

Scenarios such as this prompted automobile organizations, local police officers, Ontario government officials, and local residents to clamor for punishments beyond a measly fine or a seven-day jail sentence. George S. Henry, minister of public highways for Ontario, made his thoughts known at a meeting of the Essex County Automobile Club in

1928. "We have no sympathy with drunk drivers ... Any man who drives while intoxicated becomes, in my judgement, an irresponsible character," declared Henry. William Price, Ontario's Attorney General, agreed with Henry's sentiments. A few months after Henry's proclamation, Price issued an edict that imposed mandatory jail time for all drunk drivers. Still others wanted to see even more stringent punishment. Following the $100 fine and brief jail term of an aggressive, inebriated American driver in Sandwich, the town's Police Chief advocated for increasing the jail term for drunk drivers to 60 days.[421]

Drunk drivers also created significant issues on the American side of the border during the final years of prohibition. An April 1931 traffic analysis in Detroit concluded intoxication was by far the primary cause of motorcar accidents predicated on the condition of the driver. Whereas only 22 crashes were collectively caused by sleepy, disabled, or confused drivers, 123 accidents occurred due to drunk drivers.[422] Inebriated automobilists in Toledo and Detroit imperiled the lives of boys and girls and made other children orphans when their parents became victims in fatal accidents. Parked cars and pedestrians often could not escape the crooked path of Motor City motorists filled with moonshine. In the summer of 1929, a drunken joy-riding party outside of Detroit ironically slammed into the "expensive and resplendent new car" of Reverend Roland A. Holsaple, Michigan's superintendent for the Anti-Saloon League. Though the minister's vehicle was wrecked, Holsaple escaped the crash without injury and arranged an automobile ride to the local police station for the intoxicated men.[423]

From a law enforcer's perspective, intoxicated motorists on the TDW corridor presented a whole range of problems. Referring to drunk drivers in 1928, Windsor's Chief Constable stated that "they are the worst problem we have to deal with." Many local police officers would have concurred with this statement. First, the sheer number of drinking automobilists was often overwhelming and it was not uncommon for there to be several alcohol-induced accidents on a given night. More problematic and complicated, however, was the actual policing of drunk drivers. Beyond the fact that inebriated men and women could easily flee the scene if they were behind the wheel, it was quite difficult in the late 1920s and early 1930s to actually discern whether an automobilist was truly drinking.

Ontario's Attorney General alluded to this difficulty when he asserted, "police should exercise very great care in making arrests; they must be certain in their minds that a man is intoxicated and unable to control his car and is becoming a nuisance on the public highway." As indicated by this statement, law enforcement officials needed clear evidence that a driver was indeed inebriated. If they arrested motorists without collecting credible observations, the case could be dismissed in court. Doctors paired up with the Detroit police to craft techniques to detect intoxication, including checking the palms and tongues of drivers. However, these medical tests were soon discredited by local courts systems. Judge Edward J. Jefferies of Detroit declared, "You may as well throw all of these alcoholic test reports into the waste-basket, because I will not permit them on the records of my court." [424]

[399] "Get Williams Too," *Detroit Free Press*, February 9, 1928.

[400] "Four Suspects Caught After 20 Mile Chase," *Toledo News-Bee*, May 3, 1929.

[401] Orilla Durocher Sisung, interviewed by Marion Childs, July 11, 1958, in Marion Childs' Interviews, Ellis Reference Library, Monroe County Library System.

[402] Harold Stotz, interviewed by Mark Metz, January 31, 1996, Monroe County Community College Oral Histories, Monroe County Museum Archives.

[403] Marty Gervais, *The Rumrunners: A Prohibition Scrapbook*, (Ontario: Biblioasis, 2009), 126.

[404] "Runners Haul Liquor Across Frozen River," *Detroit News*, February 13, 1930.

[405] "Officer Slain by Prohibition," *Detroit Free Press*, June 5, 1930.

[406] "US Indicts 17 in Rum Probe," *Detroit Free Press*, December 13, 1930.

[407] "Four Murders Get Scrutiny of Rum Probe," *Detroit Free Press*, August 25, 1927;

[408] "Lawyer Named as Aid to Rum Ring in Monroe," *Detroit Free Press*, August 27, 1927.

[409] "Hearing Bares Vice in Monroe," *Detroit Free Press*, September 23, 1927.

[410] "Here is History of Kinsey Case," *Monroe Evening News*, May 25, 1928; "Runner Claims that $100 Freed Him," *Detroit Free Press*, September 27, 1927; "Runner Tells of Ring's Rule," *Detroit Free Press*, September 28, 1927.

[411] "Green Clears Sheriff Kinsey," *Detroit Free Press*, May 26, 1928.

[412] Ibid.

[413] "Mr. X Names Rum Barons," *Border Cities Star*, March 22, 1929; "Shimman Convicted of Liquor Charges," *Toledo News-Bee*, December 23, 1929; "Booze Bribery Reveals Scope of Bribery," *Toledo News-Bee*, January 17, 1930; "Rum Plotters Get 18 Months," *Detroit Free Press*, December 30, 1930; "Gains Dismissal on Rum Charge," *Border Cities Star*, February 5, 1931; "Czar of City' Liquor Traffic Faces Charge," *Toledo-News Bee*, April 6, 1931

[414] "2 'Honest' Rum Runners Free," *Detroit Free Press*, June 30, 1928.

[415] "Marshall Dohr Faces Recall for Rum Bribe," *Toledo News-Bee*, January 11, 1930.

[416] "Police Here to Get Equipment," *Toledo News-Bee*, April 26, 1928; "Asks Aid toWar on Rum-Running," *Lansing State Journal*, January 16, 1930; "State Orders Three Fast, Armored Autos," *Detroit Free Press*, March 11, 1930.

[417] "Ohio Motorist Asks Green to Halt Evil," *Detroit Free Press*, March 10, 1929.

[418] "Dry Agent Terrorism Protested," *Detroit Free Press*, June 3, 1928.

[419] "Border Guard Held for Shooting of Ecorse Citizen," *Detroit Free Press*, February 23, 1929; "Bullet Victim Frees Guards," *Detroit Free Press*, February 26, 1929; "U.S. Men Empty Guns at Fleeing Cars," *Detroit Free Press*, December 9, 1929.

[420] "Dry Heads Map Drive; Windsor Resents Shots," *Detroit Free Press*; "The Canadian Border," *Toledo News-Bee*, January 24, 1930.

[421] "Now," *Border Cities Star*, July 13, 1927; "Trip Along Tracks Costs Stay in Jail," *Border Cities Star*, December 14, 1927; "Essex Auto Club Envoys Aid in Move to Curb Highway Mishaps," *Border Cities Star*, May 3, 1928; "Price Asks Drunk Drivers Jailed," *Border Cities Star*, August 16, 1928; "Wild Once But Tame in Court," *Border Cities Star*, May 20, 1930.

[422] "Jaywalking Outranks Other Accident Causes," *Detroit Free Press*, June 4, 1931;"Driver Sentenced," *Toledo News-Bee*, May 13, 1931; "His Car Kills 2; Worries Over Being in Jail," *Detroit Free Press*, December 21, 1927; "Woman Killed, Driver Jailed," *Detroit Free Press*, March 26, 1928; "Two Men, Woman Die in Traffic," *Detroit Free Press*, June 25, 1928; "5 Are Injured by Wild Driver," *Detroit Free Press*, October 4, 1930.

[423] "Drunk Driver Hits Policemen's Auto," *Detroit Free Press*, March 27, 1930; "Man Suffers Minor Injuries in Collision," *Toledo News-Bee*, May 18, 1931; "Holsaple Car Wrecked, Two Men Are Held" *Detroit Free Press*, May 7, 1929.

[424] "Thirty Days for Drunk Drivers Proposed," *Border Cities Star*, October 23, 1928; "Magistrate Warns Detroiters They Must Obey Laws," *Border Cities Star*, February 24, 1930; "Six in Crashes Sent to Jail," *Detroit Free Press*, March 18 1930; "Drunk Driver Given a Year," *Detroit Free Press*, December 1, 1931; "Say Drunk Driver Fled from Scene," *Border Cities Star*, November 29, 1928; "Price Asks Drunk Drivers Jailed," *Border Cities Star*, August 16, 1928; "Drunk Driver Case Evidence Lacking," *Border Cities Star*, October 9, 1928; "Suspects Must Show Tongues," *Detroit Free Press*, May 16, 1928; "Court Bans Motorists' Drunk Test," *Detroit Free Press*, May 18, 1928.

CHAPTER 17
A Deadly Connection: Automobility & Gangland Slayings on the TDW Corridor

While drunk drivers were a growing problem, brutal gangland activities on American soil topped the list of priorities for law enforcement. It overshadowed not only drunk drivers, but cases of motorcar-related corruption, aggressive enforcement, and even the area's violent hijackings. The regional bloodlust seemed to commence on March 28, 1927 in an apartment complex on the outskirts of downtown Detroit. Machine gunfire echoed down a hallway at the Milafores Apartment, ripping apart the bodies of three men connected to the Motor City's bootlegging underworld. A number of theories were investigated and the usual suspects brought in for questioning, but the so-called Milaflores Massacre was never solved. One of the only certainties about the gruesome slaying was that automobility enabled such a crime. As confessed by one of the dying gangsters, the kidnapping of his friend by automobilized thugs set into motion the shooting. The slain men were subsequently lured into the Milaflores Apartment by promises they could pay for the release of their companion. The assassins quickly fled the scene in a vehicle parked in the back alley.[425]

Automobiles were essential tools for prohibition-era gangsters. Nowhere was this more evident than in Detroit during the summer of 1930. Between May 31 and July 28, fourteen men associated with rumrunning operations or law enforcement were slain. Of those men, eight were shot and killed in their vehicles by gunmen who were also in motorcars. Automobility not only enabled murderous assassins to leave a given crime scene quickly, but it also placed unsuspecting targets on or near roadways where they could be readily ambushed. A prime example of this occurred on July 14, 1930 when a Henry Tupancy, a known rumrunning gangster, was murdered on the Motor City's east side. Tupancy and a companion parked their vehicle on a side street not too far from the Detroit River shoreline. Soon thereafter, a "large roadster" appeared and a sharply dressed man stepped out of the car. After visiting a neighborhood drug store, the man then proceeded to walk briskly in front of Tupancy's automobile and rapidly emptied two revolvers into the rumrunner. The shooter fled the scene in the waiting roadster.[426]

The killers in two other high-profile Motor City slayings were also dependent on motorcar mobility. Jerry Buckley, a popular local radio show host—who also happened to crusade against the influence of booze racketeering and organized crime in local politics—was gunned down in a downtown hotel lobby by at least two gunmen on July 23, 1930. The unidentified gangsters quickly exited the building and jumped into an automobile parked alongside the hotel. More than a year later, members of the notorious Purple Gang perpetrated the infamous Collingwood Manor Massacre. Upset with a small group of bootleggers who began to break away from their authority and cut into tight profit margins, Purple gangsters set up what seemed to be a friendly meeting at the Collingwood Manor Apartments on the outskirts of Detroit. The three booze smugglers showed up at the appointed time and were brutally gunned down in room 211. In the alley behind the apartment complex, a Purple chauffeur was waiting in a black 1930 Chrysler coupe. As soon as the assassins descended the back stairwell, the chauffeur turned the ignition and the gunmen hightailed it into the vehicle. The gangsters' automobile peeled out of the alleyway and into the streets where witnesses reported the vehicle travelling close to 70 miles per hour.[427]

A couple months later, the downriver community was shaken to its core following the murder of one of its leading illegal beer barons, Joseph Rivetts. Rivetts, a Wyandotte resident, had been recently exonerated from the fatal shooting of Joe Evola, another downriver bootlegger who was trying to force Rivetts to buy his booze. The shooting, however, left Rivetts a "doomed man" and many locals openly discussed when he would be targeted. On the night of November 6, 1931, Rivetts decided to visit his friend's saloon, Tear's Cozy Inn, near downtown Wyandotte. Minutes after Rivetts' arrival, gangsters stormed the bar and exhausted their machine guns while a waiting automobile was intentionally

A rendering of the path of the getaway vehicle used by the gunmen Collingwood Manor massacre. (Photo courtesy Wayne State University, Walter P. Reuther Library)

backfiring just outside the door. Witnesses reported the men had fled the scene in two vehicles: a brown Studebaker sedan and a black Ford coupe. A day later, a Studebaker matching the description of the one at the crime scene was found abandoned in Detroit. Not only was the vehicle's license plate stolen, but the Studebaker itself had previously belonged to another downriver bootlegger, Charles Bishop, who was murdered just a month before. As it was clear in other gangland killings, automobility played a key role in the unsolved slaying of Joseph Rivetts.[428]

The automobility of prohibition-era gangsters also enabled them to transport the bodies of their victims to more isolated locations along the TDW corridor. Monroe County, with its vast swaths of swamps, woodlands, and farmland sandwiched between Detroit and Toledo, was an ideal place for kidnapped men to be "taken for a ride." In a yearlong period between 1926 and 1927, seven bodies of middle-aged

Thomas Yonnie Licavoli (holding the bottle), along with Norman Hauger, Jacob Firetop Sulkin, and other members of the Purple Gang, in a home in Toledo's Old Orchard neighborhood, ca 1930. (Photo courtesy the Toledo-Lucas County Public Library, Images in Time)

males were found in the area. All of their corpses had been dumped via motorcar. In early May 1928, just days before he was supposed to testify before Canadian officials looking into possible tax evasion practices, a prominent accountant who worked for various Border Cities exporters was abducted from his apartment complex in Windsor and "carried across the line in an automobile." A couple days later, the man's body was found in a heavily wooded area in Monroe County with his skull smashed in and two bullet wounds in his head. A local farm boy told detectives he witnessed an automobile in the vicinity of the body engaging in peculiar actions. The vehicle not only lingered in the area for two hours but it sounded its horn several times as if it were signaling others nearby. The Canadian accountant's murder was never solved.[429]

Arguably, Toledo was the scene of the TDW Corridor's most infamous rumrunners' war. In his book *Nothing Personal Just Business,*

CROWDS FLOCK TO SCENE OF LATEST GANGLAND MURDER

A photo on the front page of the July 17, 1931 edition of the *Toledo News-Bee* shows where the bodies of a pair of bootleggers from Cleveland were dumped. (Image courtesy the Toledo-Lucas County Public Library, Images in Time) local historian Kenneth R. Dickson vividly covers the Glass City's murderous spree spearheaded by gangster Yonnie Licavoli during the final years of prohibition. A close analysis of the fourteen gangland killings in Toledo from 1931 to 1933 demonstrates once again the underworld's dependence upon automobility to successfully "settle differences." Licavoli and his henchman mastered their use of motorcars and other advantageous aspects of automobility to commit booze-related murder.

The killing spree started on July 16, 1931 when two Cleveland bootleggers were found dead on a "lonely road" on the northern outskirts of Toledo. Their bodies were discovered "bound hand and foot" and riddled with bullets. Witnesses in the neighborhood claim seeing a large sedan speeding from the scene late the previous night, indicating the men had been driven to the location by their automobilized captors. Investigators later located an abandoned Packard Sedan a mile south of the shooting. A quick look-up of the license plate revealed that the car belonged to Harry "the Carpenter" Gertzlein, a "booze king" from Cleveland. Apparently, he and his partner, Al Jaffe, had come to "muscle in" on the thriving beer business in the Glass City.[430]

This killing foreshadowed how Licavoli's gang would continue to manipulate unique aspects of automobility to put their rivals "on the spot." Seasoned gangsters knew that TDW motorists—criminals or not—often put their guard down when traveling about the region. Licavoli's motorized hitmen would study their target's driving routines and discern the make and model of their target's vehicle. Subsequently, the gunmen would trail the identified automobile and wait for a moment in which the driver was least suspecting a fusillade of bullets.

On October 6, 1931, a rival bootlegger left a Toledo restaurant with some gambling buddies when their vehicle came to a stop at a red light just outside of downtown. It just so happened that the motorist in the adjacent lane was a restaurant owner from Monroe County, a man they knew quite well. The Toledo bootlegger, however, did not realize Licavoli gangsters were in the small sedan behind them. While the acquaintances were exchanging pleasantries at the traffic stop, an assassin from the sedan snuck up to the rumrunner's vehicle, jumped on to the running board, and emptied his revolver into the driver and his passengers. Immediately after the fatal shooting, the gangsters' motorcar picked up the gunmen and sped away. A couple months earlier, a rival Toledo businessman traveled to a lakeshore dancing pavilion he owned in Monroe County. Witnesses reported seeing three mysterious men spying on the owner at this location. Yet, the hitmen could only watch and then trail the businessman's vehicle after he decided to chauffeur the dance's musicians to his downtown restaurant and ultimately back

A *Toledo News-Bee* diagram of the October 6, 1931 murder of Abe Lubitsky, who was shot in his car on Franklin Avenue at Bancroft Street in Toledo. (Image courtesy the Toledo-Lucas County Public Library, Images in Time)

to their hotel. The gangsters struck at the last moment, just after the rival owner parked in his garage. A witness to the murder testified that a brown 1929 Hudson peeled out from the scene with Illinois plates. A quick investigation into the license plate revealed that the Hudson had been issued to an individual with a fake name and address.[431]

Licavoli's men also took advantage of the region's vast networks of roads. Hitmen working for Toledo's booze boss frequently abducted individuals in their auto, stolen cars, or even their targets' vehicles, steering them to isolated locations to complete their deadly jobs. Rivals' corpses were sometimes found in snowdrifts or abandoned in their own vehicles on the peripheries of Toledo. Others were transported north across the Michigan state line into Monroe County. In the early summer of 1932, a small-time bootlegger promising Licavoli protection went missing. His decomposed body was found in a southern Monroe County swamp and his car had been burned by an acetylene torch, cut into pieces, and buried a couple miles away. A few months later, two Toledo rumrunners were found "bullet-riddled, strangled, and tied together" in a stolen and abandoned Lincoln sedan not far from the city of Monroe.[432]

The two most notorious slayings orchestrated by Yonnie Licavoli were also heavily dependent upon motorcar mobility. In late 1932, Jackie Kennedy—Toledo's other booze boss—lowered his beer prices to fifteen cents and subsequently witnessed a surge in his sales. Furious, Licavoli ordered his men to kill Kennedy. On the night of November 30, Kennedy and his steady girlfriend Louise Bell were enjoying a night on the town. After a fancy dinner and a show at the Paramount Theater, the couple made their way home in Kennedy's Pontiac Coupe. Driving through the Glass City and blaring popular dance tunes from the car radio, Kennedy's vehicle came to a halt at a busy intersection. Just as Kennedy leaned forward to switch gears, a tan Ford Sedan with mud-splattered plates pulled up alongside them. A continuous volley of machine gunfire echoed through downtown Toledo as the fusillade ripped into Kennedy's vehicle. Miraculously, Kennedy was left unharmed but his girlfriend's temple was pierced by one of the bullets. Bell was pronounced dead at nearby St. Vincent's Hospital.[433] Just seven months later, Kennedy was strolling with a new girlfriend near his Point Place cottage. Neighborhood residents became suspicious of three men in a maroon-colored sedan stalking the area. With Kennedy and his date in their sights, the vehicle suddenly halted and two men exited with guns. They pushed the girl aside and filled Kennedy with eleven bullets. The

Death Ride Auto and Scene of Newest Beer War Murder

The auto in which Peter Gagastino was taken for a ride and shot to death and the lonely spot off Glendale avenue where the murder occurred are shown here. Inset are the slain men, Pete Dagastino, at the left, and Domonick Mighiore.

Peter Gagastino was "taken for a ride" and murdered along with Domonick Mighiore in a field off Glendale Avenue, Toledo. The photos are from the August 4, 1932 edition of the *Toledo News-Bee*. (Image courtesy the Toledo-Lucas County Public Library, Images in Time)

sedan quickly pulled up to the crime scene, picked up the gangsters, and sped off.[434]

Yonnie Licavoli, his henchmen, and many other gangsters throughout the TDW corridor were ultimately convicted for their violent exploits, but the damage had already been done. Both the prohibition law and those responsible for its enforcement were tarnished. Prominent and ordinary citizens increasingly voiced their concerns about being caught in booze-related crossfire on regional roadways, being "taken for a ride" by menacing gangsters, or even hit by drunkards returning from Canada or a nearby speakeasy. Numerous letters to the editor from local residents poured in to area papers and newspaper editorials themselves indicated declining support for dry laws. "Are the dangers from gunfire on the river more frequent than the dangers people on the streets of Detroit encounter? The source of all such danger is from criminals and officials," declared one Michigan resident.[435] Another Michigander rightfully claimed that the "bootlegger and the criminal industry have organized as never before in history," arguing that immediate modification or repeal of the Eighteenth Amendment was the only solution to the problem.[436]

Following the onslaught of Licavoli killings, the *Toledo News-Bee* ran a series in which they interviewed both prominent and ordinary Glass City citizens about what they would do to halt the murderous spree. Many demanded drastic reforms to the Toledo Police Department and the existing dry laws.[437] A *Detroit Free Press* editorial alleged that some of the area's prohibition officers were "not much less dangerous to the public than the bootleggers and hijackers they are supposed to curb."[438] Thomas P. Henry, a Detroit native and president of the powerful American Automobile Association (AAA), lambasted dry agents for shooting at motorists in the name of prohibition. "The enforcement of a statute does not justify the killing or maiming of a single motorist," proclaimed Henry.[439] Other AAA officials argued that automobile tourism between Canada and the United States at the Detroit-Windsor border would be significantly reduced if indiscriminate shootings continued.[440]

[425] "War Declared by Gamblers, Assert Police," *Detroit Free Press*, March 29, 1927; "Gambler Alive Police Assert," *Detroit Free Press*, March 30, 1927; Paul R. Kavieff, *The Purple Gang: Organized Crime in Detroit, 1915-1945* (New York: Barricade Books, 2000) 41-46.

[426] "Fourteen Names Listed in Recent Detroit Slayings," *Detroit Free Press*, July 28, 1930; "Thug Slain in New Rum War Here," *Detroit Free Press*, July 15, 1930.

[427] "Paul Buckley Denounces Police Head," *Detroit Free Press*, July 27, 1930; "$100,000 Raised to Balk Return of Pizzino as Buckley Slayer," *Detroit Free Press*, August 12, 1930; "3 Killed by Gang; 5 Jailed," *Detroit Free Press*, September 17, 1931.

[428] "Thugs Massacre 3 in Wyandotte Saloon," *Detroit Free Press*, November 7, 1931; "Car Yields Massacre Trail Clew," *Detroit Free Press*, November 8, 1931; "Massacre Raids Made," *Detroit Free Press*, November 8, 1931.

[429] "Here is History of Kinsey Case," *Monroe Evening News*, May 25, 1928; "Windsor Man Found Slain Near Toledo," *Border Cities Star*, May 5, 1928; "Discover Clue in Rum Killing," *Detroit Free Press*, May 8, 1928; "Marsh Reveals Murder," *Toledo News-Bee*, November 22, 1926.

[430] "Two Gangsters Slain in Toledo by Rum Rivals," *Toledo News-Bee*, July 17, 1931.

[431] "Abe Lubitsky and Pal Slain in Gang War," *Toledo News-Bee*, October 7, 1931; "Night Club Owner Shot as He Balks at Holdup," *Toledo News-Bee*, August 7, 1931; "Police Arrest Marks Suspect," *Toledo News-Bee*, August 8, 1931; "Chet Marks' Death Spurs Suspect Hunt," *Toledo News-Bee*, August 10, 1931; Kenneth R. Dickson, *Nothing Personal Just Business...*, (Lesher Printing: Fremont, 2006) 56-56.

[432] "One Slain as Beer War as Beer War Flares Here; Second Man Shot," *Toledo News-Bee*, August 4, 1932; "Kennedy Gangster Found Murdered; Body Thrown from Car in South End," *Toledo News-Bee*, December 12, 1932; "Fear Skeleton Is Toledoan's," *Toledo News-Bee*, August 1, 1932; "Two Gangsters Slain in Toledo Booze War," *Toledo News-Bee*, December 30, 1932.

[433] "Gang Murders Toledo Girl, 24, As Beer War Flares in Street," *Toledo News-Bee*, December 1, 1932.

[434] "Kennedy Riddled at Point Place," *Toledo News-Bee*, December 7, 1933.

[435] "Who's to Blame for Enforcement Deaths?" *Detroit Free Press*, July 26, 1931.

[436] "Trace Cause, Effect of Dry Law Mess," *Detroit Free Press*, April 3, 1932.

[437] "Better Police Generalship, or Secret Six Idea Suggested by Toledoans to End Gang Era," *Toledo News-Bee*, December 14, 1932.

[438] "The Complain is Widespread," *Detroit Free Press*, June 4, 1928.

[439] "AAA Chief Asks Curb on Dry Men," *Detroit Free Press*, July 1, 1929.

[440] For public discontent with prohibition related crime, dry laws and enforcement also see "Catching the Small Fry," *Detroit Free Press*, August 6, 1930; "The Prohibition Report," *Toledo News-Bee*, January 15, 1930; "Voted for Prohibition; Now Wants Referendum," *Toledo News-Bee*, January 14, 1930; "Death Guns of Take Heavy Toll in Detroit During Prohibition Era," *Detroit Free Press*, December 18, 1932; "Would Put Law on Drunken Driver," *Detroit Free Press*, March 22, 1931; "Widow of Gang Victim and Girl Friend Brave Underworld's Threat of Death to Tell What They Know of Murder," *Toledo News-Bee*, December 13, 1932; "Ghoulish Laughter," *Detroit Free Press*, April 30, 1929; Anne Marie Bonifacio to Alan Davidson, *Monroe County Oral History Project*, March 2, 1983.

CHAPTER 18
Taken For a Ride:
The Demise of Prohibition

Despite the mounting criticism levied at the prohibition law and its enforcers, Henry Ford remained unwavering in his support of the Eighteenth Amendment in its final years. His company assisted in the capture of liquor violators in the region and claimed that sobriety rates among Ford's factory workers had risen dramatically.[441] The prominent industrialist also shared his ardent views with nationally syndicated magazines and leading newspapers. In a 1930 interview printed in *The Ladies Home Journal*, Ford emphatically declared that prohibition was good for the economic outlook of the nation. He argued that both industrial administrators and workers alike would be negatively affected by the reintroduction of liquor into American society. "We must choose between drink and poverty on the one hand, and Prohibition and prosperity on the other...There is no middle ground," assured Ford. In another interview with the Pictorial Review, Ford warned that an American future with alcohol would be a future without his services. "For myself, if booze ever comes back to the United States I am through with manufacturing," Ford stated. "I would not be bothered with the problem of handling over two hundred thousand and trying to pay them wage which the saloons would take away from them. I wouldn't be interested in putting automobiles in the hands of a generation soggy with drink."[442]

Henry Ford, however, no longer represented the standard view many automobile magnates held regarding the Eighteenth Amendment. Historians of prohibition have pointed out that America's greatest financial crisis was a major driving force behind the repeal movement. As the Great Depression ravaged the national economy—including causing a sharp decline in automobile sales—potential tax revenues from regulating the liquor industry and booze-related jobs became a focal point of wet arguments. Accordingly, some of the leading motorcar moguls connected to the TDW corridor reversed their positions on prohibition, recognizing perhaps that the additional revenue collected from liquor sales would lessen the corporate taxes that their businesses were suffering from.

"I feel [prohibition's] repeal would have a good effect on banishing the depression. We lose so much money from the taxes we don't collect," asserted John N. Willys, the owner of Toledo's Willys-Overland Motor Company.[443] Alfred P. Sloan, CEO of General Motors, declared, "lawlessness will no longer be subsidized and as a very important and vital economic consideration, industry will be relieved from part of the heavy burden of taxation through an increase in Government revenue made possible by placing the sale of liquor under governmental auspices." Harvey Firestone, the Ohio-based tire manufacturer and supplier of Ford Motor Company, also decided to come out in favor of repeal in 1932 due to economic concerns. Firestone's reversal was particularly surprising, considering the fact he was one of the original sponsors of the Eighteenth Amendment, a staunch defender of the dry platform, and a close friend of Ford.[444]

Henry B. Joy, owner of the Packard Motor Company in Detroit, turned against prohibition for entirely different reasons. An active member of the Anti-Saloon League early on, Joy witnessed firsthand why so many ordinary TDW corridor residents had joined the fight in favor of repeal. Joy's St. Clair Shores residence became a dry battleground multiple times during the final years of prohibition. At first, Joy was frustrated with the number of trucks and motorcars loading up liquor around his lakeside property. Soon, however, dry agents began to engage

Hamtramck motorists protest prohibition in downtown Detroit in 1932. (Photo courtesy Wayne State University, Walter P. Reuther Library)

in shootings with rumrunners around Joy's house. On one occasion, federal agents spotted bootleggers transferring booze into a truck and decided to chase the smugglers on to Joy's private property. The officers even kicked down the door of one of Joy's boathouses, but the destructive search was fruitless. The automobile magnate ultimately concluded, "I cannot myself protect my premises against use by smugglers or marauding federal officers. Of the two I would rather be visited by the smugglers because they have done my premises no damage."[445]

With his influence and firsthand experience, Joy became a leading figure in the movement to repeal the Eighteenth Amendment in the region and beyond. He helped organize and motivate wet organizations such as the Association Against the Prohibition Amendment (AAPA) and the Crusaders, attracting both ordinary citizens and notable businessmen.[446] His wife, Helen, became the outspoken director of the Michigan branch of the Women's Organization for National Prohibition Reform, which grew exponentially during the final dry years. Prohibition proponents mounted an all-out campaign to preserve the Eighteenth Amendment, publishing reports, editorials, studies, and statistics that supported keeping dry laws intact. Nevertheless, Joy could see that the drys' stubbornness would eventually lead to their demise in political circles and society as a whole. In a published statement criticizing a national enforcement report that favored ramping up dry efforts, the automobile executive argued that such a report ignored the "rising tide of protest" that supported immediate repeal. The only "remedy" for such obstinacy, in his estimation, could be found in the ballot box. Voters in Michigan and throughout the country, Joy claimed, would soon "replace the prohibitionists in public office in the national government and in our state government [with] practical common sense advocates of temperance and wise government."[447]

Henry Joy's statement foreshadowed the near future. Dry politicians in Michigan, Ohio, and throughout the country lost elections at record rates in the early 1930s. The Anti-Saloon League's membership plummeted and the great influence it once wielded quickly disappeared. Prohibition was soon repealed with the passage of the Twenty-first Amendment in 1933 and, not surprisingly, Michigan was the first to ratify the landmark legislation. Ironically, motor trucks delivered legal kegs of beer and crates of liquor on so-called "Repeal Day" in Detroit, Toledo, Monroe, and other communities along the TDW corridor. Henry Ford, the ardent prohibitionist, recognized his last-ditch efforts and warnings were futile. In an apparent attempt to rebrand himself and the Ford Motor Company, the 70-year-old carmaker surprisingly served beer at a luncheon in 1933 while also unveiling the newest automobiles in the Ford line.[448]

Henry Ford and other drys had used the argument "gasoline and booze don't mix" to justify their unpopular support of the Eighteenth

Following the repeal of Prohibition, workers unload the first legal cases of beer in the Motor City, fittingly from the back of a truck. (Photo courtesy the *Detroit News*)

Amendment, clearly suggesting that drinking in the age of the automobile was problematic and even dangerous.[449] Most citizens residing along the TDW corridor concurred with these sentiments, but to many this argument missed the larger point. Local residents directly experienced how state and national dry laws, in and of themselves, resulted in problematic and dangerous circumstances. Prohibition not only fomented a set of conditions that were conducive to profitable, violent criminality, but the Volstead Act was also nearly impossible to enforce.[450]

Often overlooked by historians, the rapid rise of a motorcar culture greatly contributed to the lawlessness that characterized the prohibition era. Nowhere was this more evident than along the TDW corridor. Besides possessing a ready source of high quality booze in Canada, the region's deep connection to mass automobile production ensured that its residents were steeped in motorcar culture and adept with the steering wheel in their hands. In turn, the area's automobilized smugglers were quite numerous and innovative when transporting their illegal cargo. Regional dry enforcers, in order to keep pace with their rumrunning rivals, felt compelled to engage in questionable and even life-threatening policing practices.

In the late 1920s and early 1930s, booze-related, gangland killings and police corruption scandals became intertwined with regional motorcar culture. By that time, it was clear that prohibition did not "mix" well with anything, especially the large motoring populace inhabiting the TDW corridor. The "noble experiment" failed dramatically on this narrow, though important strip of territory that encompassed two nations, two American states, numerous towns, villages, and cities, and a people inclined to enjoy intoxicating beverages. Prohibition was "taken for a ride" on the TDW corridor and the region's motorcar culture was a driving force behind its ultimate demise.

[441] "Drys Capture Whiskey Fleet," *Detroit Free Press*, February 11, 1927; "Dearborn is Now Dry as a Bone, Ford Motor Officials Announce," *Detroit Free Press*, June 11, 1930; "Sees Ford Men Drinking Less," *Detroit Free Press*, May 3, 1930;

[442] Three Interviews on Prohibition", Box 5, Accession 1023, Henry Ford Imprints, Benson Ford Research Center, Dearborn, Michigan.

[443] "John N. Willys Urges Repeal of Dry Law as Aid to Business," *Toledo News-Bee*, June 14, 1932

[444] Larry Engelmann, *Intemperance: The Lost War Against Liquor*, (New York: Free Press, 1979), 204; "Firestone Out for Dry Repeal," *Toledo News-Bee*, June 15, 1932.

[445] Larry Engelmann, *Intemperance: The Lost War Against Liquor*, (New York: Free Press, 1979), 102-103, 194.

[446] "Joy Assails Prohibition Amendment," *Detroit Free Press*, October 16, 1930.

[447] Ibid.; "Open Branches of Crusaders," *Detroit Free Press*, October 20, 1930; "Dry Repeal Drive Started by 50,000 Michigan Women," Larry Engelmann, *Intemperance: The Lost War Against Liquor*, (New York: Free Press, 1979), 206-207, "Sees Failure in Dry Report," *Detroit Free Press*, January 23, 1931.

[448] "Mr. Ford Reveals for 1934," *Border Cities Star*, December 7, 1933.

[449] "Ford Makes New Attack on Booze," *Detroit Free Press*, August 22, 1929.

[450] "Drys Assail Disregard of Volstead Act," *Border Cities Star*, April 26, 1926; Harry S. Warner, *Prohibition: An Adventure in Freedom*, (Westerville, Ohio: American Issue Press), 1928, 220-222.

REFERENCES

Primary Sources

"1916 Vernon's City of Windsor Directory," SWODA: Windsor & Region Publications.

American Issue, Anti-Saloon League Museum, Westerville Public Library, Microfilm

American Issue (Michigan Edition), Bentley Historical Library, University of Michigan

Amherstburg Echo, 1912 -1918, http://ink.ourdigitalworld.org/wer.

"Auto Drivers' Licenses," *The Indicator,* vol. 45, August 5, 1919.

"Automobiles Instead of Rum," *Brewers Journal and Barley Malt and Hop Trades' Reporter,* (New York City: New York), October 1, 1916.

"Barbour's New Idea Directory of Wyandotte, Ford City, and Grosse Ille, and Farms on Mail Routes," 1921, Bacon Memorial District Library, Wyandotte, Michigan.

Border Cities Star, 1893-2019, https://www.newspapers.com/title_10943/the_windsor_star/

Brown, Ames. "Nation-Wide Prohibition", *The Atlantic Monthly* 115, 1915.

"Bulk of Larcenies are Automobiles", *Detroit Motor News,* vol. 1, July 1918, 19.

"Car Thefts Boost Insurance Rates," *Motor World for Jobbers, Dealers, and Garagemen,* vol. LX, August 27, 1919.

Circuit Court Archives. Monroe County Courthouse, Monroe, Michigan, Microfilm.

Chicago Tribune, 1849-2019, https://www.newspapers.com/title_4351/chicago_tribune/

Dearborn Independent, Benson Ford Research Center, Dearborn Michigan.

"Detroit Don'ts," *Automobile Journal*, vol. 64, 1917.

Detroit Free Press, 1913-1933, https://www.newspapers.com/title_3676/detroit_free_press/

"Detroit Thefts Most," *Motor Age*, vol. 34, June 26, 1919.

Elser, Frank. "Keeping Detroit on the Water Wagon." *The Outlook,* (April 2, 1919): 560-562.

"Editorial." *Michigan Food and Drug Monthly*, April 1919

Einstein, Izzy. *Prohibition Agent No. 1*. New York: Frederick A Stokes Co., 1932.

Emmet, Boris. *Profit Sharing in the United States.* Washington: Government Printing Office, 1917.

Evansville Press, 1906-1927, https://www.newspapers.com/title_4060/evansville_press/

Fitch, John. "Ford of Detroit and His Ten Million Dollar Profit Sharing Plan", *The Survey*, vol. 31, 1915.

Ford Times, Benson Ford Research Center, Dearborn, Michigan.

Ford Motor Company Archives, Box 91, Accession 285, Benson Ford Research Center Dearborn Michigan.

Ford Motor Company Archives, Box 106, Accession 285, Benson Ford Research Center Dearborn Michigan.

Gardner, H.W. "Windsor, Ontario, 1913, Canada: Including Walkerville, Ford, Sandwich and Ojibway," 1913. SWODA: Windsor & Region Publications. https://scholar.uwindsor.ca/swoda-windsor-region/24

General Letterbook, 1903. Thomas A. Edison Papers Digital Edition LB-069 http://edison.rutgers.edu, accessed October 12, 2017.

"Giving Motor Cars the Final Road Test in Driveaways," *Automobile Journal*, vol. 65, June 10, 1918

"Helpful Hints and Advice to Employees: To Help Them Grasp the Opportunities which are Presented to Them by the Ford Profit-Sharing Plan" *Ford Motor Company*, 1915.

Henry Ford Imprints, Box 5, Accession 1023, Benson Ford Research Center, Dearborn, Michigan.

"Henry Ford Points the Way to Other Leaders in Industry in Prohibition of Intoxicants in His Plant" *Manufacturers Record*, Volume 82, Issue 2, December 7, 1922.

"H.T. Talbot's 1928 Auto Road Atlas of the United States and Eastern Canada," author's personal collection.

Huron Valley Sentinel, The Huron Valley Sentinel Newspaper Project, Flat Rock Historical Society, http://flatrockhistory.org/archives/the-huron-valley-sentinel-newspaper/

"Ingenious Devices Employed by Whisky Runners." *Michigan Food and Drug Monthly*, (March 1919): 22-24.

 Lee, John R. "The So-Called Profit Sharing System in the Ford Plant" *Annals of the American Academy of Political and Social Science*, Vols. 63-65.

Mandel, Arch. "The Automobile and the Police", *The Annals of the American Academy of Political and Social Science*, vol. 116, Issue 1, pp. 191 - 194.

Marvin Sharpe Reminisces, Benson Ford Research Center, Dearborn, Michigan.

"Maumee Village Directory," June 1, 1927, Toledo-Lucas County Public Library Local History Archives, Toledo, Ohio.

"Maumee Village Directory," June 15, 1929, Toledo-Lucas County Public Library Local History Archives, Toledo, Ohio.

Monroe Evening News, Monroe County Local History Collection, Microfilm, Ellis Library, Monroe, Michigan.

Monroe County Oral Histories, Monroe County-Ellis Public Library, Monroe, Michigan.

Muncie Evening Press, 1905-1996, https://www.newspapers.com/title_4976/muncie_evening_press/

"Municipal Statistics: Report on Cities and Towns Having a Population of 10,000 and Over," Ottawa: Dominion Bureau of Statistics, 1920.

New York Times, 1920-1933. https://www.newspapers.com/title_395/the_new_york_times/

"No Breath of Rum in the Ford Works." *Literary Digest* vol. 74, September 30, 1922.

Oregon Daily Journal, 1902-1922 https://www.newspapers.com/title_3349/the_oregon_daily_journal/

Perrysburg Journal, Online Newspaper Archive Way Public Library, Perrysburg, Ohio, http://way.advantage-preservation.com/

Pittsburgh Post-Gazette, 1877-2005, https://www.newspapers.com/title_3518/pittsburgh_postgazette/

"Register of Arrests: From July 1, 1918 to September 5, 1918." Central Station: City of Toledo, Toledo Police Department Safety Building Attic, Book 39.

"Report of a Crime Survey." *Toledo City Journal* VI, No. 5 (January 29, 1921): 49-55.

Riggs, Henry Earle. "Reports of the Problems of Traffic and Transportation in Toledo." *Toledo City Journal.* December 1925.

Salt Lake Herald, 1906-1920, https://www.newspapers.com/title_1672/the_salt_lake_heraldrepublican/

"Shall the Automobile be Prohibited." *The Wine and Spirit Bulletin*, vol. 30, 1916, 67.

Sheboygan Press, 1904-2019, https://www.newspapers.com/title_3732/the_sheboygan_press/

Smith, F.L. "War on the River", *The Outlook*, July 24, 1929.

Sorenson, Charles. *My Forty Years with Ford*. New York: Norton, 1956.

"Story of a Studebaker Six," *Insurance Newsweek* vol. 21, 1920.

Tarbell, Ida. *New Ideals in Business: An Account of Their Practice and Their Effects Upon Men and Profits*. New York: MacMillion, 1916.

Temperance or Prohibtion? New York City: The Hearst Temperance Contest Committee, 1929.

"The Automobile Champion, Henry Ford, is Heard on Breweries", *The American Brewers' Review*. Volume 31, 1917.

"The Downriver Directory," 1915, Bacon Memorial District Library, Wyandotte, Michigan.

"The Ford Plan for Employees' Betterment", *The Iron Age* vol. 93, 1914.

"The Saloon and Industrial Works", *The Iron Age* vol. 93, 1914.

The Ohio Motorist. Cleveland: Cleveland Automobile Club, 1917.

Toledo Blade, Local History and Genealogical Archives, Toledo Lucas County Public Library, Microfilm.

Toledo Chief of Police Miscellaneous Papers, Ward M. Canaday Center, University of Toledo

Toledo News-Bee, Google News Archive, https://news.google.com/newspapers?nid=k_8v9Q84L5sC

"Toledo Leadership: Manufacturing in Toledo," 1929, in Toledo Industries Pamphlets Folder, Monroe County Museum Archives.

Toledo Police Department Miscellaneous Records, Ward M. Canaday Center, University of Toledo

"Toledo's Reorganized Police Force," *The National Police Journal*, March 1919.

U.S. Congress. Senate Committee on the Judiciary. *Brewing and Liquor Interests and German Propaganda*, 65th Congress, 2nd Session, 1919.

"U.S. Makers Build Plants in Canada," *The Automobile*, vol. 36, June 21, 1917.

Warner, Harry S. *Prohibition: An Adventure in Freedom*. Westerville, Ohio: American Issue Press, 1928.

Walter S. Mallory Letterbooks, June-July 1894.Thomas A. Edison Papers Digital Edition, LM- 222, http://edison.rutgers.edu, accessed October 12, 2017.

Windsor Evening Record, 1912 -1918, http://ink.ourdigitalworld.org/wer.

Wilder, Rose Lane. *Henry Ford's Own Story: How a Farmer Boy Rose to the Power that Goes with Many Millions, Yet Never Lost Touch with Humanity*. New York: Forest Hills, 1917.

"Willys Overland in Full Production," *Automotive Industries*, vol. 40, June 26, 1919.

"Women Working in Factories," *The Automobile*, vol. 36, June 28, 1917.

Wyandotte Herald, 1913-1933, Bacon Memorial District Library, Wyandotte, Michigan.

"Youths Form Club to Steal Cars," *Automobile Topics*, vol. 32, December 27, 1913.

Secondary Sources

Anderson, Lisa. *The Politics of Prohibition: American Governance and the Prohibition Party, 1869–1933*. New York: Cambridge University Press, 2013.

Anderson, Matt. "Ford's Five Dollar Day," January 3, 2014, retrieved from https://www.thehenryford.org/explore/blog/fords-five-dollar-day/

Baldwin, Neil. *Henry Ford and the Jews: Mass Production of Hate.* New York: Public Affairs, 2001.

Behr, Edward. *Prohibition: Thirteen Years that Changed America.* New York: Arcade Publishing, 1996.

Binder, John. *Al Capone's Beer Wars: A Complete History of Organized Crime in Chicago During Prohibition.* Amherst, New York: Prometheus Books, 2017.

Blum, Peter H. *Brewed in Detroit: Breweries and Beers Since 1830.* Detroit: Wayne State University Press, 1999.

Brode, Patrick. *Dying for a Drink: How a Prohibition Preacher Got Away with Murder.*

Biblioasis: Windsor, 2018.

Bryan, Ford R. *Friends, Familes & Forays: Scenes from the Life and Times of Henry Ford.* Detroit: Wayne State University Press, 2002.

Crawford, Richard. "Local Effort to Make San Diego Dry Was All Washed Up," *San Diego Union-Tribune,* February 24, 2011 accessed at http://www.sandiegoyesterday.com/wp-content/uploads/2011/03/Anti-Saloonists1.pdf

Comte, Julien. ""Let the Federal Men Raid": Bootlegging and Prohibition Enforcement in Pittsburgh." *Pennsylvania History: A Journal of Mid-Atlantic Studies* 77, no. 2 (2010): 166-92.

Daley, Matthew. "City of Mass Production: Building, Managing, and Living in Detroit, America's First Automobile Metropolis, 1920-1933." PhD. Dissertation: Bowling Green State University, 2004.

Daley, Matthew. "The Endless Hangover: Toledo, Ohio and the Long Term Impact of Prohibition, 1930-1950." Paper presented at the American Historical Association National Conference, Washington, D.C., January 2004.

DeWindt, Edwina. *Proudly We Record: The Story of Wyandotte, Michigan*, Wyandotte Rotary Club, 1985.

Dickson, Kenneth R. *"...Nothing Personal, Just Business..." Prohibition and Murder on Toledo's Mean Streets.* Fremont, OH: Lesher Printing, 2006.

Engelmann, Larry. "Booze: The Ohio Connection, 1918-1919," *Detroit in Perspective: A Journal of Regional History*, 2 (Winter 1975), 123.

Engelmann, Larry. *Intemperance: The Lost War Against Liquor.* New York: The Free Press, 1979.

Engelmann, Larry. "O Whisky: The History of Prohibition in Michigan," PhD Dissertation, University of Michigan, Ph.D, 1971.

Gervais, C.H. *The Border Police: One Hundred and Twenty-Five Years of Policing in Windsor.* Newcastle, Ontario: Penubra Press, 1992.

Gervais, Marty. *The Rumrunners: A Prohibition Scrapbook.* Ontario: Biblioasis, 2009.

Hallowell, Gerald A. "Prohibition In Ontario, 1919-1923." Ottawa: Love Printing Service Ltd. 1972.

Hawkins, Arnette. "Raising Our Glass: A History of Saloons in Toledo, 1880-1919." Master's Thesis: University of Toledo, 2004.

Heitmann, John A. *The Automobile and American Life.* Jefferson, North Carolina: McFarland & Company, 2009.

Heron, Craig. *Booze: A Distilled History.* Toronto: Between the Lines, 2003.

Holli, Melvnin. *Reform in Detroit: Hazen S. Pingree and Urban Politics.* New York: Oxford University Press, 1969.

Jean, Caroline and Sarah W. Tracy. *Altering American Consciousness: The History of Alcohol and Drug Use in the United States*, 1800-2000. Amherst, Massachusetts: University of Massachusetts Press, 2004.

Jones, Marnie. *Holy Toledo: Religion and Politics in the Life of "Golden Rule" Jones.* Lexington: University of Kentucky Press, 2015.

Kavieff, Paul R. *The Purple Gang: Organized Crime in Detroit, 1915-1945.* New York: Barricade Books, 2000.

Kyvig, David. *Repealing National Prohibition.* Chicago: University of Chicago Press, 1979.

Illman, Harry R. *Unholy Toledo: The True Story of Detroit's Purple-Licavoli Gangs Take-Over of an Ohio City.* San Francisco: Polemic Press Publications, 1985.

Leland, Ottlie and Minnie Milbrook. *Master of Precision: Henry M. Leland.* Detroit: Wayne State University Press, 1966.

Ling, Peter J. *America and the Automobile: Technology, Reform and Social Change, 1893-1923.* Manchester: Manchester University Press, 1990.

Loomis, Bill. "1900-1930: The Years of Driving Dangerously." *Detroit News,* April 26, 2015. Accessed June 16, 2017. http://www.detroitnews.com/story/news/local/michigan-history/2015/04/26/auto-traffic-history-detroit/26312107/

Mason, Phillip. *Rum-Running and the Roaring Twenties: Prohibition on the Michigan-Ontario Waterway.* Detroit: Wayne State University Press, 1995.

McGirr, Lisa. *The War on Alcohol: Prohibition and the Rise of the American State.* New York: W.W. Norton, 2016.

McMurray, David A. "The Willys-Overland Strike, 1919." *Northwest Ohio Quarterly* 36: no. 4 (Autumn 1964).

Meyer, Stephen. *The Five Dollar Day: Labor Management and Social Control in the Ford Motor Company, 1908-1921.* Albany, New York: State University of New York Press, 1981.

Murdock, Katherine. *Domesticating Drink: Women, Men, and Alcohol in America, 1870-1940.* Baltimore: Johns Hopkins University Press, 1998.

Norton, Peter. *Fighting Traffic: The Dawn of the Motor Age in the American City,* Cambridge: MIT Press, 2008.

Naldrett, Allen. *Lost Car Companies of Detroit*. Charleston: The History Press, 2016.

Okrent, Daniel. *Last Call: The Rise and Fall of Prohibition*, New York: Scribner, 2010.

Palmer, Brian. "How Did Detroit Become Motor City?" *Slate*. February 12, 2012. Accessed June 16, 2017. http://www.slate.com/articles/news_and_politics/explainer/2012/02/why_are_all_the_big_american_car_companies_based_in_michigan_.html

"Population of the 100 Largest Urban Places: 1910 and 1920," *U.S. Bureau of the Census*, accessed at https://www.census.gov/population/www/documentation/twps0027/tab15.txt

Powers, Madelon. *Faces Along the Bar: Lore and Order in the Workingman's Saloon, 1870-1920* (Chicago: University of Chicago Press, 1998.

"Factory Development is Setting Fast Pace," The Windsor Evening Record, April 9, 1912;

Roberts, David. *In the Shadow of Detroit: Gordon M. McGregor, Ford of Canada, and Motoropolis*, Detroit: Wayne State University Press, 2006.

Robinson, J. Lewis. "Windsor, Ontario: A Study in Urban Geography," M.A. Thesis, Syracuse University, 1942.

Ruth, David E. *Inventing the Public Enemy*, (Chicago: University of Chicago Press, 1996).

Rumbarger, John. *Profits, Power, and Prohibition: Alcohol Reform and the Industrializing of America, 1800-1930*. Albany, New York: State University of New York Press, 1989.

Scharff, Virginia. *Taking the Wheel: Women and the Coming of the Motor Age*. Albuquerque: University of New Mexico Press, 1992.

Schneider, John. *Detroit and the Problem of Order, 1830-1880: A Geography of Crime, Riot, and Policing*. Lincoln, Nebraska: University of Nebraska Press, 1980.

Timberlake, James. *Prohibition and the Progressive Movement.* London: Cambridge University Press, 1963.

Tracy, Doug. "May 1, 1918: The End of Vice in Toledo, Ohio, Detective Tracy, Madam Nellie Schwinn and Life in the Tenderloin." (unpublished).

Thompson, Neal. *Driving with the Devil: Southern Moonshine, Detroit Wheels, and the Birth of NASCAR.* New York: Random House, 2006.

Watts, Steven. *The Peoples' Tycoon: Henry Ford and the American Century.* New York: Vintage Books, 2005.

Williams, LeRoy. "Black Toledo: Afro-Americans in Toledo, Ohio, 1890-1930." Dissertation Ph.D. University of Toledo, 1977.

INDEX